The Counselling Approach to Careers Guidance

The counselling approach to careers guidance allows clients to develop a clearer understanding of themselves and the wider issues affecting their career choices. Through detailed case material Lynda Ali and Barbara Graham demonstrate how to use counselling strategies to enable clients to change unhelpful patterns of thought and to move towards achievable goals.

The Counselling Approach to Careers Guidance offers a structured model which can be adapted to meet the specific needs of every client. Each of the four stages is illustrated with examples of good practice, showing how to establish the purpose of the interview, the counsellor/client relationship, the key issues for the client and the options available. Using this approach the counsellor is able to help the client move towards a realistic plan of action and to provide the client with the means and the motivation to continue the process independently.

The book also explores materials available to careers counsellors and includes a discussion of important issues affecting training and development of advisers in the public sector.

This will be a useful handbook for experienced advisers and trainees, in the careers service and a range of professional settings.

Lynda Ali is Senior Careers Adviser at Edinburgh University. **Barbara Graham** is Director of the Careers Service, University of Strathclyde. **Susan Lendrum** is author of *Gift of Tears* and *Case Material and Role Play in Counselling Training* and a counsellor in private practice, Manchester.

The counselling approach to careers guidance

Lynda Ali and Barbara Graham

Edited by Susan Lendrum

Routledge
Taylor & Francis Group

LONDON AND NEW YORK

First published 1996
by Routledge
27 Church Road, Hove, East Sussex, BN3 2FA

Simultaneously published in the USA and Canada
by Routledge
270 Madison Avenue, New York, NY 10016

Reprinted 2000

Reprinted 2003, 2004 and 2007
by Routledge
27 Church Road, Hove, East Sussex, BN3 2FA
270 Madison Avenue, New York, NY 10016

Routledge is an imprint of the Taylor & Francis Group, an informa business

© 1996 Lynda Ali and Barbara Graham

Typeset in Times by Florencetype Ltd, Stoodleigh, Devon
Printed and bound in Great Britain by CPI Bath

This publication has been produced with paper manufactured to strict environmental standards and with pulp derived from sustainable forests.

British Library Cataloguing in Publication Data
A catalogue record for this book is available from the British Library

Library of Congress Cataloging in Publication Data
A catalogue record for this book has been requested

ISBN: 978-0-415-12173-6

Contents

Acknowledgements

The authors wish to acknowledge the assistance of the many people who have had a hand in the writing of this book. In particular we are grateful to the guidance practitioners who were our own role models as we were learning about our profession and beginning to practise the counselling approach to guidance. Our editor, Susan Lendrum, and our typist, Helen Crossan, helped the book to grow and develop with their patient contributions to the shaping of the text.

We also acknowledge the assistance of the Advice, Guidance, Counselling & Psychotherapy Lead Body in allowing reproduction of a chart showing links between these various fields.

Chapter 1

Introduction to counselling in careers guidance

In a world in which the concept of 'a career' is becoming increasingly fluid, careers guidance is not a once-in-a-lifetime injection of wisdom which orients a person in a particular direction for all time. As life enters new phases and external circumstances add fresh dimensions to a person's situation, so the need for guidance arises at various times in an individual's life.

Because the need for guidance is associated with uncertainty about future steps, people who seek guidance may regard it as a remedy for a crisis and may expect a ready-made solution from the lips of an expert. Guidance practitioners, on the other hand, recognise guidance as a process to be worked through by the client over time, with support and encouragement from the careers adviser.

Since there is potential for the two participants in a careers interview to approach it with such divergent expectations, it is vital that the adviser should make the client aware at an early stage in the discussion of the respective roles of the client and the adviser. It is also important to clarify what can and cannot be achieved during a careers interview. This book therefore begins with a definition of guidance and a look at the people involved in giving and receiving it.

WHAT IS GUIDANCE?

Effective careers guidance is a process which aims to equip individuals with a clearer understanding of themselves and their potential for future career development. In particular, careers guidance helps individuals to:

- assess their career development needs at various points in their lives;
- understand the process of effective choice of a career;
- clarify their objectives for the future;
- take appropriate action to implement these objectives.

People who are approaching a decision about their future often benefit from speaking to a skilled and informed listener, who can help them to put the many factors affecting their career development into perspective so that they can choose an appropriate direction for the next phase of their lives.

WHO GIVES GUIDANCE?

Careers guidance is not the exclusive preserve of careers officers in the Careers Service and careers advisers in higher education. A recent study[1] has shown that the most influential factor in young people's choice of degree course is advice from parents. Other informal sources of advice include friends, employers, teachers, librarians, community workers and voluntary agencies such as the Citizen's Advice Bureaux.

Some of the advice from these sources may be sound, well-researched and appropriately targeted, but this is not always the case. Because such 'advice givers' are not specialists in careers work and may deal with careers enquiries infrequently, the advice which they give may be, at best, limited and, at worst, out of date, erroneous and misleading. Despite these limitations, informal sources of advice will continue to be used for careers guidance, perhaps because of their very accessibility. The challenge to guidance practitioners is to try to be equally accessible and to demonstrate the benefits of well informed professional careers guidance. Through their contacts with employers, careers advisers are in a unique position, enabling them to interpret, for jobseekers, employers' recruitment needs and their expectations of applicants. This knowledge anchors their advice in an appreciation of the real world of work which may not be apparent to their clients.

Every individual – irrespective of age and ability to pay – should be entitled to up-to-date, accurate, unbiased careers information and guidance delivered by trained, competent, professional guidance practitioners. This ideal has not yet been translated into reality, although it is close to being achieved for learners in schools and universities and the situation is improving in further education since charters for further and higher education pointed out students' right to careers guidance alongside other basic entitlements. For adults outside of education, however, provisions are extremely patchy and access to sound careers guidance may depend upon geographic location, ability to pay or the fortunate coincidence of working for an enlightened employer with a strategy for the career development of staff.

It is therefore worth clarifying the sources of help on careers issues to which people in the post-16 age group can turn with the expectation of receiving professional guidance. The following list also represents the target audience for this book.

GUIDANCE PRACTITIONERS

The term 'guidance practitioner' covers the following groups of people:

- Careers officers employed in the Careers Service within local authorities, or, following reorganisation of the Careers Service, local enterprise companies or training and enterprise councils.
- Careers advisers in higher education institutions.
- The growing number of careers advisers in further education institutions.
- Careers counsellors in private practice.

Although the settings and circumstances in which they work may differ in certain respects from those of the groups mentioned above, other practitioners are also involved in some aspects of careers guidance. These include:

- Careers and guidance teachers working with pupils over the age of 16 in schools.
- Educational guidance workers who help adults to select courses which will have a direct bearing on their future career planning.
- Out-placement counsellors dealing with people whose jobs are redundant.
- Personnel managers who specialise in the career and management development of members of their workforce.
- Guidance specialists in training agencies who help their clients to choose training courses appropriate to their future career aspirations.

This book is about good practice in guidance, and will be of interest to students, probationers and trainers involved in training for the Careers Service as well as those who are directly responsible for advising clients in a whole range of professional settings.

WHO RECEIVES GUIDANCE?

While guidance may be associated primarily with people who are setting out on a career path after leaving education or those who have been forcibly evicted from their employment by redundancy, the need for guidance can occur for anyone at any time. The following are among the groups of people who can be identified as guidance seekers and whose case histories will be encountered in this book:

- People leaving education at secondary or tertiary level.
- People wishing to return to education in order to improve their employment prospects, acquire new skills or update their knowledge and skills after a career break.
- Returners from career breaks who wish to know about options open to them in resuming or changing their careers.
- People whose jobs are redundant or insecure.
- Workers who are achieving little job satisfaction and want to find more rewarding employment.
- People whose jobs are too stressful or have become too demanding physically.
- Staff whose hopes of promotion have not been fulfilled and who want to stimulate their career development by being pro-active.
- People who want to switch from full-time to part-time work and vice versa.
- People contemplating setting up their own business.
- Older workers who are approaching retirement, but want to find meaningful occupations in the broadest sense, which will lead to self-fulfilment and a sense of being valued by the community.

The guidance needs of all of these people and the timescales in which they want to operate vary, but they have in common a need to:

- take stock of their present circumstances;
- understand the factors influencing their decision making;

- appreciate more realistically what they have to offer;
- review and evaluate the options available to them;
- identify preferred options;
- formulate an action plan which will result in the achievement of their objectives.

The primary purpose of guidance is to assist individuals in their exploration of these complex issues, to make greater sense of their current situation and to build confidence in their ability to complete the review process and move forward from the point at which they seek help.

ADOPTING A COUNSELLING APPROACH

All of the people described above are encountered by guidance practitioners at a time when they are going through or are on the brink of a major transition – literally moving from one state of being to another. The decisions which they make about themselves in relation to work or education – or the absence of these activities – often have a significant impact on other aspects of their lives and the people around them. Effective careers guidance therefore cannot be given in a vacuum. It must take into account the life circumstances in which the next phase of a person's career will be set.

It is this approach to the whole person which distinguishes the work of the skilled guidance practitioner from that of givers of information on careers. In order to function in this way, a careers adviser will find it helpful to focus on an individual client's needs by using a counselling approach to guidance which is built upon a highly developed, inter-related set of communication skills. Used appropriately, these skills can help free a client from unhelpful patterns of thought and facilitate progress towards a solution both within and beyond the time spent together in the interview.

The counselling approach also distinguishes careers advisers from other professionals who are concerned with the interface between people and work (e.g. personnel officers, recruitment consultants and occupational psychologists). Whereas these other specialists are primarily concerned with the selection, training and maintenance of an effective, skilled workforce for an organisation, the focus of the careers adviser is on the individual, with a view to helping him or her to find the most appropriate career path out of all the options which are available. The careers adviser is aided in the discussion by knowledge of the needs of the labour market, but also contributes to the interview a greater understanding of human development and how people respond to others. The adviser can also help the client by finding parallels between the skills and temperament required for specific occupations and the client's self-description of his or her abilities and personality.

HOW THIS BOOK IS STRUCTURED

The next chapter explores some fundamental questions about the nature of the counselling approach to careers guidance. What is meant by counselling skills and how do they work in careers guidance? What attributes enable careers advisers to use the counselling approach? What are the distinctive features of counselling in the careers guidance context? When is it appropriate to make referrals to other counsellors?

Chapter 3 gives a succinct overview of some theories of occupational choice and of counselling which have influenced the model of counselling in careers guidance described in this book. The theories are related to problems which clients commonly encounter and are linked to specific case studies which follow in other chapters. This chapter also outlines key influences which affect a client's outlook on life and his decision on career options.

Chapter 4 offers an integrated model for a practical approach to counselling in careers guidance. The four-stage model demonstrates how a guidance practitioner can assess and prioritise a client's needs, and draws upon theories of counselling and occupational choice in order to provide a client with a framework for exploration of career issues and options before reaching a well-reasoned decision and constructing a realistic action plan.

Chapter 5 then shows how the range of skills is actually used when applying the model. Each skill is defined and illustrated by examples from relevant situations, and ways in which careers advisers can develop these skills are explored.

Chapter 6 demonstrates certain strategies which careers advisers can use to help clients with specific difficulties to become 'unstuck' and to move forward through the phases described in the model. The examples given show how a careers adviser can employ the various counselling skills identified in Chapter 5 in order to achieve the desired outcome of a particular strategy.

Chapters 7 and 8 examine the impact of external circumstances on clients who seek guidance, focusing first on their immediate family and social circle and second on social and economic factors which have a bearing on individuals and their potential career development. Brief case studies demonstrate ways of working which take these background circumstances into account.

Chapter 9 looks at various tools which the guidance practitioner can use within the model. These include pencil and paper exercises, computer-aided guidance, aptitude tests, personality questionnaires, practice interviews, contact with practitioners in occupations and the wealth of written and video careers information to which the clients have access. It also considers ways of working with tools which enhance the client's responsibility.

Chapter 10 follows the case history of one client, Carol. It outlines her life experiences, including sociological and psychological influences, and explores her previous experiences of guidance which have coloured her later experiences. Taking Carol's 'world' into account at the moment of a university careers guidance interview, this chapter then outlines the process with the client from the counsellor's perspective. The dialogue between the client and counsellor is presented, together with the dilemmas and decisions the counsellor has to face as the interview progresses.

Chapter 11 examines important issues regarding the training and support of guidance practitioners. These relate to both initial training in counselling skills and the development of expertise in the counselling approach through a careers adviser's continuous professional development.

Finally, at the end of the book readers are given the means of pursuing further their interest in counselling in careers guidance via useful contact addresses and a select bibliography.

A NOTE ABOUT TERMINOLOGY

'Guidance practitioner' and 'careers adviser'. These terms are both used to describe people who give careers guidance in a professional capacity. These primarily include people for whom giving guidance is a main function but, within specific contexts, the term guidance practitioner is also used to refer to other professionals (for example, personnel officers) for whom careers guidance is a partial but none the less important remit.

'The client'. In the contexts which we describe, the individual seeking help may be referred to as a student, pupil, worker, graduate or client. The word 'client' has been used throughout to cover all these terms, although we are aware that it is not in common use in some settings.

'The interview'. The exchange which occurs between the adviser and the client is described in a number of ways, depending on the setting – e.g. discussion, appointment, consultation, interview. None of these seem quite right – 'consultation' confers an 'expert' status on the adviser, and 'discussion' implies a certain lack of purpose. 'Interview' has unfortunate connotations of selection, but this has been chosen as the most appropriate and most commonly used term in this context.

GENDER

Advisers and their clients may be male or female. In the examples in the book, we have sometimes used 'he' and sometimes 'she' to describe them – and in most situations the positions could equally well have been reversed, except in circumstances which tend to apply more to men or to women.

A COMMONSENSE APPROACH TO COUNSELLING

The aim of this book is to try to remove any mystique from counselling in careers guidance. In the spirit of this philosophy, the authors have tried to keep the text free of jargon and circumlocutions so that readers can concentrate on the concepts described and the potential application to their own work without any additional impediments of language. Although the issues encountered in careers guidance are often complex and interwoven, the key skill of a guidance practitioner is to clarify all the important factors for a client and to communicate options for consideration.

The strength of the counselling approach to guidance is that it enables the practitioner to work alongside the client, taking into account individual needs, abilities and expectations in the context of the labour market. The following chapter explores in some detail the nature of the counselling approach to careers guidance.

Chapter 2

The counselling approach

THE CONCEPT OF COUNSELLING IN A CAREERS SETTING

Counselling and guidance clearly share aims of enhancing self-understanding and communicating appropriate options for the next phase in a person's life. The differences between them are largely those of function and can perhaps be understood through the use of an analogy. The relationship between counselling and guidance is rather like that between a navigator and a pilot, who both have an important role to play in a ship's voyage. The navigator's job is to ensure that the ship does not get lost in the high seas, but keeps heading in the right direction for its home port. When the ship approaches the harbour, however, it is the pilot who takes over to steer it safely into dock. Both of these roles are vital, but they must happen in the proper sequence. The captain will not be receptive to detailed landing instructions while the ship is still being buffeted by gales in mid-Atlantic, but in the later stages of the voyage pays close attention to the pilot's detailed knowledge of the sand bars and currents around the harbour.

The same pattern occurs in a person's voyage through life. The skilled helper must recognise which kind of support is most appropriate for a client at a particular moment. It is pointless to bombard a client with detailed information on training courses and closing dates for applications, or even to attempt to help the client to choose one career in preference to another, if there are deeper issues such as low self-esteem and a perception of insuperable obstacles which are preventing the client from moving forwards. In such a situation the counselling approach to careers guidance can help the client to navigate the deeper waters of self-understanding in the context of his circumstances before negotiating a channel which will lead to a specific career.

Occasionally, the complexity of a person's circumstances or the nature of the individual's reaction to them makes it desirable that the first phase of self-disclosure should be facilitated by a trained, experienced personal counsellor. In many situations, however, a skilled guidance practitioner with a counselling orientation can enable the client to explore his needs and make sense of the context in which a career decision is being made. In this case the guidance practitioner is acting as both navigator and pilot, gauging what kind of support is most appropriate for the client at various stages in the discussion, but throughout the interview she continues to use counselling skills.

This concept of linked professions using common skills has been described graphically in a diagram designed by the Advice, Guidance, Counselling & Psychotherapy Lead Body (Figure 2.1).

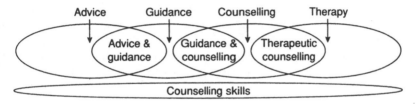

Figure 2.1 The chain of activities

COMPARISONS BETWEEN GUIDANCE AND COUNSELLING

Similarities between guidance and counselling

The person-centred approach

Both careers counselling and many other forms of activity using a counselling approach are *person-centred*. Whereas a personnel officer conducting a selection interview will be consciously assessing an interviewee against a pre-determined standard in order to decide whether the person meets the needs of the organisation, the focus of a careers adviser is entirely different. The aim of a careers interview is to help the client to move towards the best possible options out of all those realistically available. Even if an initial assessment tells the adviser that the client appears poorly qualified, personally unattractive, temperamentally unstable or unlikely for other reasons to appeal to employers, dismissing the client as being beyond hope is not an option for the careers adviser. A careers adviser with a counselling approach will try as far as is humanly possible to be aware of personal prejudices, to set these aside and to accept individuals for what they are – and could become – without sitting in judgement.

Although the purpose of a careers interview is to focus mainly on an individual's choice of occupation or change of career direction, it shares with all counselling interviews a common aim: to give a client a greater sense of control amidst a complexity of life developments. For some clients seeking help with career choice, the other aspects of their lives may be relatively harmonious. They have roofs over their heads, no more than average financial problems and support from at least some people in their lives whom they can trust. The discussion with the careers adviser can then concentrate primarily on the careers issues. In the case of other clients, however, the career issues may be swamped by other complex issues which may need to be resolved first, either through the deeper understanding of the careers adviser or through work with a personal counsellor. Referral to a personal counsellor is discussed later.

Confidentiality

As in all relationships in which one party is encouraged to trust the other, *confidentiality* must be assured in exchange for that trust. In careers guidance, this issue is much more important to some clients than to others. In many cases, no issues are raised which the client would not freely mention to anyone who was interested. The careers adviser, however, should still regard the details of the conversation as confidential. Other clients may be less trusting about the confidentiality of the interview. This distrust may express itself, for instance, through the client checking several times in the course of the interview that the fact that she is seeking other employment while still in a job will not come to the ears of her current employer. The careers adviser may then need to repeat the initial assurance that the conversation will go no further than the adviser's office. It may perhaps be appropriate to explore the theme of trusting those in authority.

In some circumstances, it may be necessary for an adviser to discuss the client's situation with a third party. If such intervention seems desirable, the appropriate action is for the adviser to propose this to the client, pointing out the benefits likely to be gained by the involvement of a third party. Wherever possible, the client can be supported in making direct contacts, but when it seems more appropriate for the adviser to intervene, this should be done only with the client's consent. Only in exceptional cases should the principle of confidentiality be overruled – for instance, where an adviser has a real concern for the safety of the client or for the consequences on other people of proposed illegal action. On the whole, however, careers counselling rarely raises issues which cannot remain confidential between the client and the adviser.

Distinctive features of careers counselling

While there are many similarities between the use of counselling skills in careers guidance and in other areas, there are certain distinctive features which differentiate careers guidance from other areas. The differences originate partly in clients' expectations of what a careers interview will be like. Many clients expect a careers interview to be a very factual discussion, leading to clear-cut career choices.

Some of the distinguishing aspects of careers interviews are outlined below.

Career issues are not problems

Many of the topics which clients bring to counsellors may be regarded by both parties as being 'problems'. This could apply to alcohol and drug abuse, debt, homelessness, breakdown in marital relations, phobias and a whole range of other issues.

In the case of occupational choice and career development, while the client may see his or her uncertainty and confusion as a major 'problem', the careers adviser tends to see the matter not as a problem, but as an issue to be discussed, explored and resolved as part of that person's development – if not in the initial interview, then at least within a reasonable timescale. This approach gives a very positive tenor to most careers interviews, with a view to encouraging the client to cease regarding occupational choice as a problem, but rather to see it as a developmental event which occurs at various turning points in a person's life.

Timescale and pace of interviews

Careers advisers in the public sector often meet their clients on only one occasion. Despite the limitations imposed by the single interview, careers advisers have to be aware that occupational choice is a process which may unfold over a long period of time. A careers interview can be an important catalyst in that process, but it is usually one of many influential factors from which a final decision is distilled.

A skilled practitioner can use the discipline of a limited timespan in a positive way within a careers interview to give it a very clear structure out of which important personal decisions can emerge.

1   In order to use time most effectively, it is important that time constraints are clarified early on in the interview. How much time is available and what is it realistic to hope to achieve in that amount of time? Once these constraints have been made clear, then other topics may arise. These can either be referred to other forms of assistance (e.g. the careers information room or direction to another counsellor), or the topic for the interview can be renegotiated according to the client's priorities within the allotted time.

2   The timekeeping is then the responsibility of the careers adviser, who must nevertheless try to ensure that the interviewee does not feel rushed through the process of exploring all the issues to be discussed. A skilled careers counsellor is one who has mastered the art of letting the client feel a sense of space about the interview, while at the same time managing the contracted time.

3   Since there is no guarantee that the interviewer and interviewee will meet again, it is essential that time is set aside within the conversation for a final summary by either the careers adviser or, ideally, the client of what has been discussed and clarified and what action the client will now take to carry forward the agreed plan. It should be possible for the client to carry out the plan independently, possibly through referral to other sources of help.

Creative use of time in the careers interview will be explored in much greater detail in Chapters 6 and 10.

The careers adviser's remit

While there are good reasons for a careers adviser to be aware of various personal issues in a client's life in order to put career options into an appropriate perspective, this does not mean to say that the careers adviser will pursue all of the issues which may emerge in conversation. If necessary, the adviser may need to reiterate the terms of the original contract, pointing out that while all the issues are important to the client, there are only some which can be tackled effectively in a careers interview. There are two very good reasons why more intensive counselling would be inappropriate. Most careers advisers have not been trained as counsellors. While they may nevertheless learn to employ counselling skills within the parameters of their own expertise, it would be unprofessional for the adviser to trespass into areas of counselling in which he has neither sufficient knowledge nor experience. It is therefore important that the guidance practitioner should try to be aware of the point in a conversation at which a referral to another counsellor might be appropriate and of how a smooth referral can be made without the client feeling like an unwanted parcel which is being posted elsewhere.

Further, the careers adviser's remit is to advise clients in relation to occupational choice, further study, job search skills and alternative career options. If an adviser were to become more deeply involved with personal issues over an extended period of time, it could only be at the expense of offering more directly relevant help to other clients. The adviser would need to use referral skills to seek further appropriate help for the client.

Sometimes, however, a careers adviser can suddenly find himself precipitated into a more personal area of the client's life – as for instance, when a phrase or a question in a dialogue triggers off an unexpected outburst of anger or a flood of tears from the client. This type of response is less unnerving for the adviser when he recognises that such a reaction may be entirely appropriate at this stage in the client's exploration of feelings below the surface and may indicate the client's recognition of what has been bottled up. It is often sufficient for the careers adviser to stay with the client, waiting for the outburst to run its course. It is then up to the adviser to gauge whether it is necessary or appropriate to explore which factors in the client's circumstances have evoked such emotions.

By summarising the significance of such an incident and agreeing this with the client, the careers adviser can bring the client to a point in the interview at which the two can decide whether it is appropriate to continue the conversation about the more personal issues raised and relate them to their significance for career planning, or agree to refer the client to a personal counsellor with more relevant training and experience.

It is important also for the adviser to remember that what happens after a career counselling session is the responsibility of the client. If the client chooses to take no action or to act in a way entirely different from what was agreed at the end of the interview, that is her prerogative. Such an outcome does not diminish the professionalism of a careers counsellor if the interview has been conducted competently and any inconsistencies in the client's behaviour and thought patterns have been highlighted and challenged.

Thus, competent performance by an adviser in a careers interview cannot necessarily be gauged by the action which the client takes after the interview – although the two may frequently be inter-connected. The adviser must therefore remain sufficiently objective to be able to evaluate the competence of his conduct of the interview in terms of effective use of counselling skills irrespective of the client's actions after the encounter.

REFERRAL

Careers advisers spend a high proportion of their time acting as signposts – referring clients to materials, information and practitioners who can help them to piece together a more detailed picture of suitable options. Referral of clients for personal counselling on issues which lie outside the careers adviser's remit can be seen as an extension of that practice. Doing so is in no sense a rejection of a client, but rather a recognition of how various types of counsellors can work together in a partnership, with each recognising the other's expertise. An account of the stages of an effective referral may help guidance practitioners to carry out the process in a way which enhances the relationship with the client. Practical illustrations of referrals are given in Chapter 6.

Recognising the need for a referral

This is the point at which it becomes clear that the adviser is approaching the boundaries of her knowledge and expertise. When in practice the adviser uses phrases like 'I would have to check that ...' or 'This may not be current practice ...', it could be that there is someone with more appropriate expertise to whom the client could speak, such as a different careers adviser or someone in a totally different field. Recognising the need for a referral in the emotional sphere may be more complex.

If, for instance, a client keeps returning to discussion of a fragile or broken relationship and cannot concentrate on the careers issue which is ostensibly the reason for seeing a careers adviser, then the adviser may feel it is appropriate to point out that little progress is likely to be made with the career search until the more predominant issue of the relationship has been discussed with a counsellor from Relate (the former Marriage Guidance Council) or other appropriate organisation.

Being aware of other counsellors and agencies

Some types of referral may occur so infrequently that the careers adviser may have to start tracking down the appropriate person after the need has arisen. Other sources of help may be used more frequently – for instance, the Citizen's Advice Bureau, a welfare rights officer, the Student Health Service – and it is therefore more efficient and less daunting to a client if the adviser has this information ready to hand in a card index or on computer. The ready availability of such information not only saves time, it also reassures the client that referrals of this kind are normal practice.

Raising the issue of referral

Sometimes the subject of referral comes up very naturally in conversation or may even be raised as a suggestion by the client. In other instances, however, the need for a referral may emerge gradually during the interview, particularly in the emotional sphere. It may then be necessary to broach the subject of referral sensitively if the impression is that the client has not yet discussed these problems with anyone else. The best way to approach the issue may be with a series of tentative questions in the direction of referral. For instance:

- 'I wonder if it would be better to try to resolve the issue of whether or not you will be leaving your wife/husband before making a final decision about changing your job?'
- 'I understand your dilemma, but helping you constructively with this kind of problem is beyond my expertise. Would it be helpful if we could identify someone who is trained in this type of counselling and who may therefore be of more use in this particular area?'
- 'Here is a contact person and telephone number for Relate counselling. Do you want to make the call yourself now or later – or would you like me to ring and make an appointment?'

If the client does not agree to the proposed line of action, the careers adviser cannot go ahead with the referral, but can leave the option open to the client to take up after reflection. The adviser is under no obligation to shoulder the burden of the client's problem because the referral has been declined.

Making an effective referral

The careers adviser should ensure that the person to whom the client is being referred knows, basically, why the referral is being made without revealing confidential details. It may be appropriate in some circumstances to ask the client to send the other counsellor a letter or further information before their interview takes place. In other situations the careers adviser may choose to brief the other counsellor – verbally or by letter.

Whenever possible, it is best to arrange a firm appointment for the client, but this is not always feasible and a brief message may have to be left on an answering machine or with someone else. In that case it is a wise precaution to give the client full details of the person with whom contact should be made if an appointment is not speedily arranged, and, if feasible, to send a memo to the other counsellor by way of confirmation.

Following up a referral

Depending on the nature of a counselling referral, it may be helpful for the careers adviser to arrange to see the client again or at least be prepared to receive feedback via a telephone call or a letter from the client. This expression of continuing interest in the client reassures him that he can continue to refer to the careers adviser about matters appropriate to career choice and job search, even though another helper may be more appropriate for other matters. A reporting back session also helps the careers adviser to judge whether the time is now ripe for a careers interview or for further referrals to untangle other issues.

COUNSELLING SKILLS

What are counselling skills?

The various guidance areas outlined above are rendered more effective through the use of counselling skills. The notion of allied professionals using common skills in their work with clients is strengthened by a closer examination of what constitutes *counselling skills*. Skilled guidance practitioners will recognise most of the following activities as part of their normal practice in conducting careers interviews:

- active listening;
- reflecting;
- paraphrasing;
- summarising;
- questioning;
- making statements;
- using silence;
- being 'real' or 'concrete';
- challenging or confronting;
- immediacy;
- self-disclosure.

Guidance practitioners using the skills within a counselling approach to guidance offer a model of effective practice in helping clients to help themselves. The skills are defined and illustrated in a guidance context in Chapters 5, 6 and 10.

When is it appropriate to use counselling skills in careers guidance?

It will be clear that the basic counselling skills outlined above are not to be kept in a box and brought out in emergencies when a 'difficult' client appears. These skills are the outward expression of the careers adviser's whole orientation towards all clients in the careers interview. They become easier to use through constant practice, until they become more or less automatic.

The sections which follow indicate the various stages of an interview in which the skills are employed.

Assessing the situation

At the outset, it is important for the careers adviser to *listen* to the client's full story and *probe* for further information if some of the client's proposals seem inexplicable at first. At this stage the adviser should *clarify* which issues can be covered in a careers interview and which areas need to be worked through elsewhere.

Counselling skills are vital in the *assessment* stage of the interview (described in more detail in Chapter 5) in which the careers adviser is laying the foundations of the helping relationship. The following questions may need to be explored:

- What are the important issues for this person today?
- What is the client's self-image?
- Does the client have a clear vision of a future direction?
- What factors might help the client to move in this direction?
- What factors might hinder the client's progress?
- What are the client's expectations of the outcome of the interview?

Until these areas have been fully explored, it is pointless to rush in with advice and information as these might be irrelevant to the client's circumstances. Counselling skills enable the adviser to complete the assessment stage of the interview. The outcome of the assessment determines the way in which the careers adviser decides to continue the interview thereafter. Depending on the careers adviser's assessment of the facts which might have emerged, it may be appropriate to adopt any one of three helping modes – providing information, guidance or counselling at a deeper level – each of which incorporates a range of counselling skills.

Providing information

If the interviewee appears to have fairly clear goals, but does not know how to proceed towards them, the basic need will be for advice in the form of information from the careers adviser. This would be the case if the client presented the following kinds of questions:

- 'How can I become a speech therapist?'
- 'Am I likely to get funding for postgraduate study in the USA – and from what sources?'
- 'Which recruitment agencies might help me to find a more senior post based on my previous experience of sales and marketing?'

The advantage to the client of discussing this information with a careers adviser is that the adviser can use counselling skills to point out parallels or contradictions between what the client has said about herself in the assessment stage of the interview and the requirements for an occupation which she is considering.

Specific guidance

It may be the case that the client is trying to reach a decision on the best of several options. The adviser's help in that instance may take the form of guidance in looking at the pros and cons of each option and enabling the client to make an informed choice.

Trigger statements or questions which would evoke this type of response from a careers adviser might include the following:

- 'I don't know if I would be better suited to news or magazine journalism – or maybe even being a reporter in broadcasting. How can I decide?'
- 'Some aspects of social work appeal to me – but I might take everybody's problems home with me. How else can I help people without wearing myself out emotionally?'
- 'When I'm dealing directly with the public, I feel much happier, but the rest of my job I hate. What jobs could I do with my qualifications which would involve more direct people contact?'

Counselling at a deeper level

If the initial assessment suggests that there are – or could be below the surface – a number of inter-related issues which could have

a bearing on the client's occupational choice or career development, the careers adviser may opt to use counselling skills at a
deeper level in order to support the client through an exploration
of how these issues impinge on one another and on the client's
self-concept. Such an approach may be suggested by the following
questions or statements:

- 'My art teacher is encouraging me to apply to art school, but
  everyone else says that's a total waste of time. I don't know
  what to think.'
- 'Everything I do seems to fall apart. I've never been successful
  at anything so far – and yet I think I could make a go of it if
  I could just find my niche in the right job.'
- 'With my qualifications I could be doing something much better
  than this pathetic clerical job, but there's very little available
  here and I can't move because it has taken me ages to finally
  work out reliable child care arrangements.'

Whether or not the careers adviser decides to invite a deeper
understanding of the client's needs, basic counselling skills will be
used throughout the remainder of the interview. With experience,
a guidance practitioner will identify those clients for whom a
deeper understanding will be necessary before it is possible to
move into the guidance or advice modes. Numerous examples of
such situations are given in later chapters of the book in the form
of case studies, but for the moment two broad categories of clients
can be identified for whom the counselling approach is essential
if the interview is to have any significant impact on the development of their thinking:

1 Clients who appear to be more than normally concerned,
  distressed or confused by the need to make a successful occupational choice or change of career direction.
2 Clients whose life circumstances bring pressure to bear on them
  and block their view of how to make a rational occupational
  choice or pursue an effective job search.

It is the responsibility of the adviser to decide how far down
the road of deeper understanding it is appropriate to travel in
each case. The decision will depend on the level of the adviser's
skills and experience and the context in which the interview takes
place.

ATTRIBUTES OF EFFECTIVE CAREERS COUNSELLORS

Many guidance practitioners will already have developed and used effectively some or all of the skills described in this chapter. Some people appear to use these more or less instinctively and have developed them through life experience – without consciously realising that they are doing so. These are the people who appear to know how to respond appropriately to a colleague's bereavement or to support a friend at a crisis point.

It is possible, however, to describe some fundamental guidelines which are at the root of the effective employment of counselling skills.

Model appropriate effective communication

From the very start of the interview, the client is picking up clues from the adviser about how to communicate effectively. Where the client experiences from the beginning an open and direct approach, where judgement is suspended, he will be encouraged to respond appropriately and to participate more fully and openly in the process of exploration.

Being tentative to enable understanding

Whichever skill is used to respond to a client, it will be offered in a tentative and exploratory way. It is possible that the adviser may have interpreted the client's story incorrectly or that the issue being explored is particularly painful for the client. A tentative approach provides the client with the opportunity to correct the adviser's view or to decide whether he wishes to explore this issue and reinforces the sense that the adviser wants to understand without imposing her own interpretation on it. It is, however, important to be wary of being over-tentative. When the adviser is hesitant, vague, perhaps apologetic or even frightened in approach, the client may feel that the adviser is confused or may perhaps sense that the issue is too difficult for the adviser to work with. This certainly does not aid the development of empathy and inhibits the building of trust.

Being specific

When the client is expected and is encouraged to be specific, then the adviser should do likewise from the start of the interview and avoid being vague.

Being brief

It is the client's perceptions and reflections which are important. The adviser's responses should be short and to the point. Their purpose is to encourage the client to continue his story, to reflect on its meaning and to provide new insights on that meaning in order to make effective plans for the future. The attention span of any individual is limited. Brief responses encourage the client to work at his own pace and allow him greater control over the progress of the interview.

Being aware of internal responses

The skilled adviser is normally aware of her own feelings and prejudices, what influences them and from where they are derived. This awareness of her own responses enables the adviser to understand more clearly what feelings and meaning are coming from what the client says and does, and what perceptions are coming from her own outlook on life.

This awareness of feelings in the self in response to topics raised in the interview or through the adviser's reaction to the client is a natural process, and one which can be used to enhance understanding rather than being ignored or suppressed. The skilled interviewer will gradually learn how to use these processes to the client's advantage. We shall return to this important theme in the case studies in the later chapters of this book to demonstrate how the adviser's inner feelings can be acknowledged and creatively used.

SUMMARY

Careers advisers share a set of basic counselling skills with allied professionals in the occupations represented by the Advice, Guidance, Counselling & Psychotherapy Lead Body. While they use those skills in order to listen to the client's story and understand the context in which her career need is being discussed, careers advisers do not have a remit or a responsibility to help clients to come to terms with every problem in their lives, although they can encourage clients to reflect on issues which need to be resolved before sensible career planning can occur and can refer them, if appropriate, to personal counsellors who can help with that task.

The length of the relationship between a client and a careers adviser is likely to be much shorter than that in other areas of counselling. A counselling approach, using all the counselling skills outlined above and described in Chapter 5, is the most effective method of achieving change within a single interview.

It is part of the skilled adviser's art to recognise at what point in the interview it is appropriate to introduce guidance and advisory modes of discussion, so that by the end of the interview the client will be clear about a range of options and their pros and cons. She will also have the specific information required for taking the next steps in her career development. Thus, in a well-structured careers interview the adviser constantly uses counselling skills while moving imperceptibly in and out of counselling, guidance and advisory modes according to his judgement of which will best serve a client's needs at that particular moment. Chapter 5 describes these skills, and the case studies in the later chapters show this process in action. Before proceeding to these, however, we shall outline very briefly the theories of occupational choice and counselling which underpin the model presented in Chapter 4.

Chapter 3

Theoretical background to counselling

This chapter provides a theoretical underpinning for careers advisers' work with clients. It draws on theories of both counselling and occupational guidance and shows how a skilled practitioner can draw upon both of these sources to enhance her understanding of inner conflicts and external influences which may affect a client's outlook on life and ability to make rational, well-founded career decisions. Theoretical knowledge can enable a careers adviser to work in a more informed and therefore less reactive way to her observations of her client's behaviour. We shall consider some counselling theories which inform all helping relationships, then go on to indicate a range of factors which may influence a client, finishing with a brief look at the community interaction theory of occupational guidance developed by Bill Law.

As outlined in the previous chapter, the counselling approach aims to help people to help themselves and is thus focused on the personal development and growth of the individual. This psychological approach has been informed particularly by the work of Carl Rogers and his *'person-centred approach'*.[1] Rogers states that effective counselling can only occur when there is mutual recognition of respect, understanding and openness between the counsellor and the client. Rogers sums up this type of relationship as one in which there is *basic empathy* between the two parties. This basic empathy is built upon three elements which are fundamental to an understanding of person-centred counselling:

1 *Unconditional positive regard*. This attitude of mind enables the counsellor to accept that the client's feelings and outlook are

real to him and to work within that context. This does not prevent the counsellor from challenging the client to reflect on views which are blocking his development or bringing him into conflict with other people. It means, however, that the counsellor seeks to avoid being judgemental and strives to overcome her own stereotypes and prejudices when working with a client.

2 *Rapport.* In establishing rapport with a client, the counsellor communicates by verbal and non-verbal means her desire to tune in to the client's concerns, self-doubt and aspirations. This attempt to start from where the client is now and 'walk in his moccasins' can provide enormous support for a client who, for instance, might feel confused and unable to communicate with people in his immediate social circle.

3 *Congruence.* Congruence can best be described as the ability to be honest about oneself both to oneself and to others. The counsellor strives to create an atmosphere in which the client feels able to explore deep-seated personal issues, which may be coming to the surface for the first time, in the knowledge that the expression of these thoughts will not be rejected by the counsellor. At the same time, the counsellor seeks to be honest about recognition of her own emotions, even when this includes judicious use of difficult feelings (such as anger, envy or dismay) evoked by the client's behaviour.

THE CLIENT'S SELF-CONCEPT

Person-centred counselling distinguishes between the client's *self* and *self-concept*.

Self

The self is the integrated whole formed by the individual's physical, mental and spiritual being. In order to experience a sense of wholeness, the individual must be aware of the value of her unique combination of these three aspects.

Self-concept

The self-concept is the client's perception of herself in relation to the world around her. This may fluctuate according to surrounding circumstances, mood swings and state of health. It is also subject to influence by external sources. As a result of all these variable, impinging factors, the self-concept may at times be far removed from the actual self. A counselling intervention can help a client to recognise the two entities and integrate them.

The self-concept is moulded by the individual's perception of how others regard her. If, for instance, there is positive feedback from family and teachers about a child's achievements and future potential, her self-confidence may be reinforced, whereas a constant barrage of negative feedback and low expectations from others may lead to low self-esteem and a depressive self-concept. If mixed messages are received (for example, from peers and parents in the teenage years), there may be confusion in the self-concept as the individual either tries to be all things to all people, or invites conflict by building a self-concept on one set of influences which is at odds with another.

These influences on the self-concept will be described in more detail in the next section of this chapter and can be seen in the case studies described in Chapters 7, 8 and 10. Before examining these, however, it is helpful to have an understanding of Rogers' concept of 'conditions of worth'.[2] This is the observation, learned in infancy, that certain behaviours gain approval or 'positive regard' from others, while other forms of behaviour attract disapproval, censure or punishment. An example of this might be where an outward show of affection can be gained only when there is unquestioning, total obedience to a dominant parent's wishes – a behavioural pattern which can last into middle age, with potentially damaging consequences for the individual's self-concept and personal development.

In some instances the individual's sense of obligation to meet the expectations of others may result in a line of action which is contrary to her own deep-seated desires. For example, a person might yearn to follow a bohemian existence in the creative arts, but be held back by her family's strong emphasis on respectability and security. The discrepancy between the desired and the actual path chosen may lead to frustration and a lack of self-fulfilment.

On the other hand, the conditions of worth may exert such a powerful influence that they become internalised and alter the self-concept. This might result in guilt about a feeling of ingratitude to parents if an individual feels stirrings of a desire to do something contrary to their wishes. The unhappy choice in this case appears to be flying in the face of the conditions of worth (i.e. losing parental approval) or stifling natural desires in order to keep the peace.

Where an individual is able to assimilate life experiences without injury to her self-concept and in a way which positively enhances self-awareness, Rogers says that the individual experiences 'unconditional positive self-regard' – in other words, a high level of self-acceptance. Greater self-acceptance enables a client to move forward more realistically to a view of how the real self may develop to achieve its potential in the future.

R.R. Carkhuff and Gerard Egan have taken Rogers' person-centred approach and developed frameworks or models for counselling which are particularly relevant to careers counselling.

Some models for counselling interviews

Carkhuff's two-stage model[3]

Carkhuff identified an 'inward' phase of the interview, focusing on the client's self-exploration, and an 'outward' phase during which a likely direction for the future emerges. Movement between these two phases is facilitated by the counsellor's expression of empathy for the client in her exploration, and ability to challenge the client when her hypotheses seem open to question. Pace and timing are important for the effective use of the model, as the counsellor must be aware of the client's readiness to move on from the first to the second stage of the interview.

Egan's three-stage model[4]

All the fundamental pre-conditions of person-centred counselling must be met in order to operate Egan's three-stage model of interviewing as a 'skilled helper'. This model's three phases can be described in terms of the goals of the counsellor and the client at each stage (see Table 3.1).

The basic tenets of person-centred counselling are also fundamental to the four-stage model of careers counselling described in Chapter 4.

Table 3.1 Egan's three-stage model

	Client's Goal	Counsellor's Goal
Stage 1: Explanation	To explain her background and her perception of the current situation. To express her needs.	To understand the client's background, perceptions and needs.
Stage 2: Exploration	To increase self-awareness and understand the influences affecting future choices. To accept the need for action and explore some options.	To integrate the client's growing self-awareness with the counsellor's objective perspective so that the client can achieve deeper understanding of both self and the available options.
Stage 3: Planning	To formulate a plan for future action based on a realistic assessment of the pros and cons of all available options.	To facilitate the client's formulation of an action plan by encouraging her to be concrete and realistic about practicalities of options.

INFLUENCES ON THE CLIENT AND HIS SELF-CONCEPT

Having thought about an approach and a model which focuses on the understanding of the self, we can also recognise the wisdom in the saying, 'No man is an island'. Each individual is subject to the influence exerted not only by other significant individuals in his life, but also by the complex interaction taking place in the society in which he is set. Figure 3.1 gives a diagrammatic impression of all the influential factors which impinge on the individual – and which should be understood by a careers adviser working with a client. The remainder of this chapter draws on theories of careers guidance psychology and social psychology to aid the reader's understanding of how various influences may impact upon individual clients.

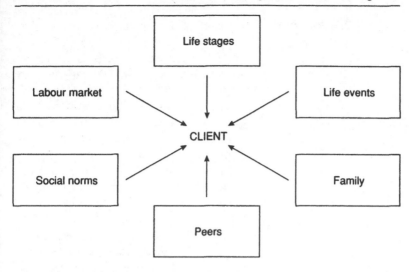

Figure 3.1 Factors influencing the client

Life stages

Donald Super has set his theory of occupational choice in the context of five life stages based around physical growth and change. These can be related to a series of career issues on which individuals may need to make decisions at different points in their lives.[5]

Stage	Characteristics
Stage 1: Growth	(Birth to age 14) The child becomes aware of being an individual and develops some degree of awareness of personal interests and capabilities.
	The child's projection of self in the future begins with fantasy notions of what he would like to become. By the end of this stage fantasy begins to be overlaid by a more realistic assessment of what might be possible in view of the child's capabilities.

Stage 2: Exploration

(ages 15–24) This stage covers adolescence and early adulthood. It is a period of intensive self-discovery on several planes, often accompanied by periods of acute self-criticism and self-doubt. Despite the development of a desire for independence there is often evidence of the need to win the approval of 'significant others'.

In terms of occupational choice, the individual is exposed to various sources of both factual and impressionistic information on careers. As experimentation with career choice develops, the individual moves closer to a realistic concept of his preferred occupational role – which may be at odds with what is actually available.

Stage 3: Establishment

(ages 25–44) This stage is associated with continuing trial of jobs to test out suitability, followed by a longer period of stabilisation during which the individual's vocational role is experienced through either advancement at work or a series of jobs.

Stage 4: Maintenance

(ages 45–64) Super describes this stage as being either one of 'fruition and self-fulfilment' if the individual has achieved earlier career goals, or one of frustration if the previous phase did not culminate in a satisfactory vocational identity. Towards the end of this phase individuals encounter the prospect of retirement and respond to it either positively or negatively.

Stage 5: Decline

(age 65 plus) Individuals react differently to this phase. Some view it as a period of freedom to develop interests, voluntary work or education for which they have not had time during their working years. Others see it only as a prelude to decay and pine for their lost vocational identity without being able to adjust their self-concept in order to recognise the value of other aspects of their lives.

While certain elements of Super's theory still seem valid several decades after he expounded it, the changing nature of the structure of work calls for the revision of the concept of 'establishment' and 'maintenance' stages for many people. Having expected to be established in a career by their middle years, many are now encountering a period of disequilibrium when they are faced with changing roles, redundancy and 'flatter' staffing structures which limit promotions.

Examples of the classic stages described by Super, as well as the upheaval experienced by individuals in the changed world of the post-Super period, are given in the case studies in Chapters 7 and 8.

Life events

As individuals develop through the stages described above, significant events can happen in their lives, causing them to reappraise their values, their self-concept and their relationship to others. These experiences include leaving home, marriage, the birth of a child, the loss of a significant person through death or other means, becoming seriously ill or disabled and a variety of other circumstances which somehow change life for the individual.

Such turning points in life require the individual to make a transition from one state of being, thinking or doing to another. Although individuals vary in their capacity to cope with change and adapt to new sets of circumstances and relationships, most people need time to work through the process of accepting change and moving on to the next stage. Adams, Hayes and Hopson[6] have identified six phases in the *transition process*, which can be seen in Figure 3.2.

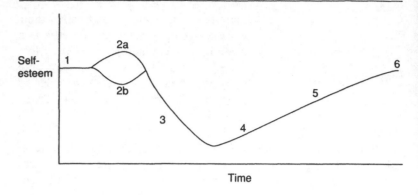

Stage	Characteristics
Stage 1: Immobilisation	The individual feels overwhelmed by the event, whether it be happy or sad. There may be a sense of disbelief and an inability to comprehend or address the consequences of the event.
Stage 2: Minimisation	Following a reaction of either elation (2a) or despair (2b), there may be an attempt to deny or minimise the impact which the event will have on the individual. This can be an initial attempt at coping and getting back to 'business as normal'.
Stage 3: Self-doubt	As the ramifications of the event are experienced, the individual may doubt his ability to cope with the transition. If this feeling is prolonged, he may sink into depression and fear that he will never again feel in control of his life.
Stage 4: Accepting reality	The individual accepts that a return to the past is not an option and that it is necessary to let go of the past and go forward to the future. This phase may be accompanied by a

	grim sense of resignation and anxiety about a future which is not yet clear.
Stage 5: Testing	This is a phase of experimentation with new behaviours and a new identity. Morale on the whole may be better, but insecurity may linger and self-doubt can easily return.
Stage 6: Searching for meaning	In this phase the individual tries to make sense of what has happened and to see how it fits into his life. He may be able to learn from the experience and apply it to future transitional situations.

Figure 3.2 The transition cycle

The theory of transition outlined in Figure 3.2 shows clearly how the past continues to have an influence on the present. It shows how apparently conscious choices made by clients may be made in the context of an underlying cycle of transition of which the individual is largely unaware. When dealing with a client who is experiencing anxiety and distressing emotions during a process of transition, the counsellor's aim is to raise the client's awareness of reality in the present. This is certainly influenced by past events, but the client can be helped to understand that what is past need not dominate all his future choices.

This theory can be related to significant events in an individual's experience of working life. For instance, any of the following turning points can cause a transitional crisis:

- entering employment for the first time;
- gaining promotion;
- changing job;
- being dismissed;
- becoming unemployed through redundancy;
- retiring.

The impact of all of these situations on individuals is examined in more detail in the case studies in Chapters 7 and 8.

Family

The psychological environment and the behavioural norms provided by the family are important, but largely unconscious influences on the individual. Eric Berne developed a matrix for interpreting these influences in his theory of transactional analysis.[7] Berne believed that an individual fluctuates between three ego states, which can be described as patterns of thinking, feeling and behaviour.

Ego state	*Manifestation*
Parent:	The individual in this state may display either controlling behaviour (bound by rules and generally prohibitive or even punitive), or nurturing behaviour (showing caring, sympathy and support for another person or for self).
Adult:	This state is marked by the ability to approach situations realistically and to assess them rationally on the basis of the information available. It is associated with the ability to adapt to change.
Child:	The individual in this state is driven by feelings and attitudes unresolved in childhood which may stem from the wishes of another. In a more positive vein, when the repressed feelings find some kind of resolution, then more natural aspects of childhood can re-emerge and be seen in expressions of spontaneity, creativity and self-nurture. In this process there may be considerable rebellion against authority figures as the 'inner child' strives to find greater independence.

In any social interaction – or transaction – each party may adopt one of these ego states without necessarily being aware of them. The outcome of a transaction depends on whether one party sees the other as a superior, a peer or a subordinate. While each individual has the capacity to move from one of these roles to another, it is possible in situations where the same roles are repeatedly adopted for behavioural patterns to become permanently fixed in one type of transaction – as, for instance, when one partner in a marriage becomes permanently dominant.

Berne believed that people conduct their lives according to 'scripts' of which they are largely unaware and which are derived from parental influences. Even when people think in their later life that they are making autonomous decisions, these mainly unconscious influences may have a strong sway over their lives. This can cause them either to suppress their natural inclinations or to feel guilty when deviating from their 'script'. When the nature of the 'scripts' can be understood, then the power of specific influences to affect decision making can be consciously recognised and dealt with more appropriately.

It is not appropriate here to discuss transactional analysis in detail, but the power of internalised parental influences and the struggle to discard those aspects of it which are inhibiting can be seen in some of the examples in Chapter 7 and in the case study which is discussed at length in Chapter 10.

Peers

Alongside parental influence, the desire for acceptance by peers has a powerful influence, particularly in adolescence. The significance of this influence is described in one of the stages of Erik Erikson's theory of psychosocial development.[8] Erikson's theory described eight life stages, but the one in which peer influence is strongest is the period of adolescence, between the ages of 14 and 20. Erikson described this as a period in which an emergent sense of individual identity clashes with role confusion as the teenager seeks to leave behind his childhood identity, which is framed in terms of 'the child of X', but has not yet classified his future identity in terms of his vocational and social role in society. This has similarities with Super's theory of life stages.

The uncertainty which is experienced during this phase may lead the young person to seek a common identity with a group of peers. As the teenager seeks to establish independence from parents or find his own identity, there may be a strong attraction to join a group of peers whose values and behavioural patterns are far removed those of the family, particularly when it may be difficult for him to find his own identity within the family framework.

When this is applied to a vocational setting, it can mean that the young person might aspire to a lifestyle which is more glamorous and financially rewarding than that of his parents.

Alternatively, he might choose to under-achieve academically in order not to be out of step with a group which prizes other forms of behaviour rather than academic achievement and perhaps because there is an underlying wish to rebel against his parents. In either case the urge to be acceptable to peers by being as like them as possible may transcend the need to clarify and follow his own individual goals and recognise both similarities to and differences from his parents.

Some people seem prepared to live with the consequences of career decisions taken at this stage throughout their lives – for instance, missing out on education and therefore being confined to unskilled work or remaining unhappy in a well-paid but unfulfilling job. Others, however, reach a stage in mid-life which Daniel Levinson in his evolving life structure theory, developed in the 1970s, called BOOM – 'becoming one's own man'.[9] Levinson described this stage as one in which 'Greater individuation allows him to be more separate from the world, to be more independent and self generating.'

Evidence of both kinds of development are found in the case studies in Chapter 7, while the longer case study in Chapter 10 describes a mature student – the classic example of an adult who decides to adopt the BOOM approach to life, but often finds it hard to let go of influences from the past.

Social norms

Beyond the influence of family and peers, there lies a complex set of social mores which specific cultures lay down in order to regulate society and to differentiate between what the majority call 'normal' and 'abnormal' behaviour. These 'cultures' may be based on nationality, ethnic origin, social class, age groups or gender. Such groups have a tendency to operate in stereotypes, and extremist defenders of the key concepts of a particular culture may discriminate against those who cannot or will not conform to the social norms.

The consequences for the individual of the power of these social influences are described in the social learning theory developed by Albert Bandura.[10] He argued that most learning occurs through observation of other people's behaviour and its consequences for the individual. The most likely outcome is that individuals will copy behaviours which they see modelled by people with whom they identify – for instance, a young woman may confine occupational choices to those occupations which she sees practised by other women. Bandura showed how an individual's perception of what is open to him beyond the social norms can be developed through what he called 'participant modelling', which enables the client to build up confidence in a concept of himself doing something which is different from the norm for his group or 'culture' in Bandura's sense.

A theory of social learning within occupational choice has been developed by Mitchell, Jones and Krumboltz.[11] This theory identifies four conditions which influence an individual's perception of realistic career options.

Factors	*Consequences*
Genetics and abilities	Physical and mental endowment rule out some occupations (e.g. eyesight deficiency for a pilot) and make others possible (musical ability for an opera singer).
Environment	Lack of social and educational opportunities or encouragement to aspire to ambitious goals may depress an individual's career expectations.
Learning experiences	The presence or absence of role models to whom an individual can relate will influence his views on what is possible for someone of his gender, social class, ethnic origin and general background to achieve.
Task approach skills	Unless an individual has learned to clarify his values, seek information, evaluate the consequences of career options, choose a preferred option and plan in order to achieve it, his sense of control over career choice will remain under-developed and he will remain passive instead of proactive in determining his career.

The careers adviser has an important role to play in ensuring that individuals who might be disadvantaged by factors such as physical disability, social environment or discrimination on grounds of gender, age or race are encouraged to think beyond these limitations and are given strategies for coping with difficulties which they may encounter. The case studies in the later chapters of this book give examples of this approach in practice, with specific strategies outlined in Chapter 6.

Labour market

Super's theory of five life stages including a long period of 'establishment' (ages 25–44) and 'maintenance' (ages 45–64), has been criticised for taking insufficient account of the economic factors which have a bearing on career choice. Super subsequently modified his theory to acknowledge the significance of 'situational determinants'.[12]

At the other end of the spectrum from Super is the opportunity structure theory of Ken Roberts.[13] Roberts' thesis is that for most people occupational choice is structured by factors outside the individual, including social class, educational opportunities and the current state of the labour market, depending on economic trends in supply and demand.

This is built into the work of an earlier theorist, P. M. Blau,[14] whose theory of the process of occupational choice and selection included a number of socio-economic factors alongside other determinants such as psychological and biological conditions. These included elements such as the rate of labour turnover, the division of labour among groups of workers, the policies of relevant organisations (including the government, firms and unions) and the stage in the business cycle at a given point in time.

While these theories may give insufficient scope for the individual who aspires and succeeds against the odds, there is a need to incorporate awareness of the labour market into any theory of occupational choice which will remain viable in the twenty-first century. The structure of work is in a period of rapid and radical change, which will result in a very different organisation of the work force. It is predicted that by the end of the twentieth century, less than half of UK workers will be full-time, long-term employees. Even the élite, highly educated and highly skilled professionals will have little long-term security, as short contracts and freelance working become more common so that organisations can keep a tighter rein on their budget. The implications of these labour market issues for individuals are dealt with in more detail in Chapter 8.

COMMUNITY INTERACTION THEORY

The strands of both the development and the opportunity structure theories come together in Bill Law's community interaction theory.[15] While recognising the powerful influence of what he calls 'organismic states' (early experiences, including the contribution of the family to the development of the individual's self-concept), he states that the community sets a standard for social interaction and can transmit motivation to an individual member – or can fail to do so.

Law's 'ragbag of community' consists of peers, neighbours, teachers and other authority figures, ethnic groups and the hierarchy of social classes. He identifies five ways in which the community influences individuals:

1 Expectations	Communicated explicitly or implicitly by family members and peers. Conflicting expectations may confuse the individual's career choice.	
2 Feedback	Reactions by others to the individual's tentative career choice confirm or deny her suitability for particular occupational roles in the eyes of the community.	
3 Support	Encouragement from sectors of the community can reinforce the individual's career choice and enable her to progress towards it.	
4 Modelling	Observation of other people in work roles helps the individual to decide whether a similar occupation might suit her. This is powerfully reinforced if the role model comes from a similar background.	
5 Information	As members of a community, individuals receive both factual data about employment and impressions gained from people in work. These can help to shape their view of the types of work available and suited to their own needs.	

The attraction of this theory is that it envisages the individual tentatively measuring occupations against her self-concept and then using the community as a source of information and feedback on the suitability of specific options. This may be a description of the ideal scenario. In reality, depending on the strength of the self-concept and the power of the influence of the community, the individual may decide to follow her own inclinations with or without the approval of the community, or she may succumb to external pressure and relinquish her own preferences.

Law envisages the careers adviser as a pro-active partner in this process of using the community as an aid to career decision making. In this theory, the careers adviser is not seen as an expert directing a passive client, as in Alec Roger's trait and factor theory, on which heavily structured the 'seven-point plan' was based,[16] but as a coordinator of the rich resources within the community which can equip a client to make a well-founded career decision. The contribution of the adviser is to help the client to establish what questions she wants to ask and to show her how to make contacts, research information, arrange work-shadowing or placements and finally set all of her accumulated knowledge of both self and an occupation within a framework in which decision making can occur.

Thus the careers adviser is a pro-active facilitator of the process of occupational choice. One can see many links between this concept and Egan's role for the 'skilled helper' with a counselling orientation. By combining these theories of guidance and skilled counselling a careers adviser can adopt a counselling approach within a careers guidance interview, during which it may be appropriate to draw upon the information, network of contacts and tools of his profession. Understanding the theories allows the adviser to recognise what is happening in an interview and this should therefore be the basis of any model of careers counselling.

SUMMARY

This chapter has described briefly some of the theories of counselling and guidance which can provide a careers adviser with a better understanding of clients and their environment. Most counselling theories have been developed from working with people who are more or less disturbed at some point in their lives. While these theories are relevant to the situations of people who seek vocational guidance, in that they can provide an under-standing of some of the less conscious influences on decision making, there is a recognised need for the development of other frameworks specific to careers counselling for a wider range of clients. The next chapter offers a model for a counselling approach in careers guidance with all clients which the authors have developed as a vehicle for effective use of counselling skills, against the background of the theoretical knowledge outlined above.

Chapter 4

The model for a counselling approach

The model we describe in this chapter is very much a personal practical approach. It is derived from both occupational choice theory and counselling theory. As a working model, it has been developed through extensive experience in the field and will continue to develop in the light of further experience. Two working counselling models have particularly influenced the development of this model – G. Egan's *Skilled Helper* and Sue Culley in *Integrative Counselling Skills in Action*.[1]

WHY DO WE NEED A MODEL?

The model is the foundation of the careers interview which provides a firm structure designed to achieve the desired outcome, namely that the client has moved on in some way along the process of career planning. Without this firm base, the interview will resemble a cosy chat, and may simply reinforce the client's mistaken beliefs about the responsibility of self or the world of work or both. Without a structure, both the client and the adviser will feel lost and flounder without direction, with a consequent raising of levels of stress and dissatisfaction for both.

An inexperienced, untrained adviser may try to operate without a model and may rush to respond to and try to fulfil the client's expectations, which are often unrealistic. Such an adviser is likely to escape into information provision, whether or not it is appropriate. As we shall see in Chapter 10, the timing and quality of information provided in a careers interview are of crucial importance. An unstructured approach does not recognise the underlying needs of the client (although there are many advisers who practise it) and it is often used when advisers have difficulty with the client who is not 'straightforward', particularly when the client has strong feelings that bubble up to the surface during the interview. The operation of a model allows the adviser to recognise important feelings, monitor progress and evaluate her own performance in meeting the objectives set for the interview.

Usually an adviser will develop her own particular model, based on theoretical reading, the models of other professionals in the field and the practical experience in her own work setting. Any such model is not static and will continue to develop throughout the adviser's professional life.

The model described here is a process model, and as such reflects the process of career planning. The careers interview itself is also part of that process. It is unrealistic to imagine that a careers interview will resolve all issues of choice for the client and these very expectations may increase stress on the adviser. What the adviser is aiming for is an intervention which will both motivate the client to continue the process and demonstrate a methodology for doing so.

The model consists of a series of phases which reflect the process of career and life planning. As particular issues emerge during the interview, the adviser will explore some of these by introducing the model within the overall process.

This concept will be illustrated in more detail at a later stage in this chapter.

The shape of the model in any one interview will depend on the needs and circumstances of the individual client, together with the time available for and the setting of the interview. For some clients the first stage will take a high proportion of the interview time; for others – including those who have returned for a subsequent session – the evaluating and action planning stages will dominate. Whatever the individual shape, the adviser should aim to complete the model in its entirety in each interview, by careful monitoring and pacing throughout the interview period. The approach is person-centred, whilst the skilled adviser manages the session by allowing various loops of exploration while maintaining an overall sense of the shape of the model and requirements of the process.

Advisers who are just beginning to introduce counselling skills into their practice often express anxiety about losing control of what goes on. Basing the interview on a structured model ensures that the adviser manages the process, which will be explored further in Chapter 5.

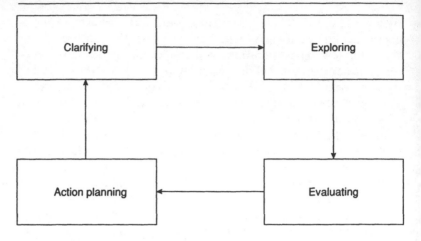

Figure 4.1 The model

The model does not stand in isolation. It has been developed through the use of counselling skills and should be read together with Chapters 5 and 10.

Figure 4.1 shows the very simple four-part model. Within each phase of the model the adviser is set a number of tasks to complete before moving on to the next phase.

THE CLARIFYING PHASE

- setting the scene;
- developing empathy;
- hearing the client's story;
- making an initial assessment.

Setting the scene

It is essential to set the parameters of the interview and to start developing empathy.

Experienced advisers may find themselves over time forgetting the importance of setting the parameters of the interview – to them the interview situation is not new and feels mechanical. For each new client, however, it is a new situation. The client does not really know what to expect from the adviser or from the interview process. It is probable that advisers make assumptions about the level of clients' knowledge of the process. A simple format will clarify for the client the timescales involved and who they are working with, and begin to establish the cooperative working relationship. For example: 'I'm Sandra. I generally work with the history students on their career plans. We have about three-quarters of an hour to work together. Can you tell me where you would like to start?'

Developing empathy

The key element running through a counselling relationship is the development and strengthening of empathy. Empathy is extraordinarily difficult to define and the conveying of empathy is a skill in itself. For the present authors it is a description of a state in which the client senses the trust, warmth and interest of the adviser in a way which enables the client to be open and to take some personal risks.

The adviser is able to put himself in the shoes of the client, to understand how she sees the world and her own emotions and to try to convey that understanding to her.

Empathy is developed and expressed through the effective employment of counselling skills. Some individuals are fortunate in possessing a natural sense of empathy, while others will have to work hard on themselves and their skills to learn this. It is of course easier to develop empathy with some clients than with others. Where we can identify with the client's situation, perhaps because we have experienced something similar ourselves, it is relatively easy to put ourselves in the client's shoes in order to establish an empathic relationship. There are inherent dangers with such identification, however, in that we may assume our experience is the same as that of others – remember, it can *never* be exactly the same. Each individual experiences the same circumstances differently, depending on her own value system derived from previous experiences.

Cultural differences can make the development of empathy a harder task. Where, for instance, an individual's upbringing has involved discouragement from even looking at a member of the opposite sex, let alone having eye contact, it can prove difficult to convey warmth and understanding. To take another example, clients with disabilities may feel an adviser could never understand what it is like to be in their situation.

In summary, empathy is hard to define, can sometimes be extremely hard work to develop, but when it exists it can be almost tangible. It must be developed from the very beginning of the counselling relationship and requires nurturing throughout the process.

Hearing the client's story

This involves allowing and encouraging the client to talk about her concerns, identifying issues which are important to her. It is facilitated by the adviser through the use of active listening skills and through paraphrasing and summarising (as described in Chapter 5). It is important for the adviser to take an active part in achieving the balance between encouraging the telling of the story on the one hand and focusing on the important issues on the other. The adviser helps the client to separate the details of the story from the messages contained in it. Inexperienced advisers can find they get stuck at this point – they have developed the basics of empathy but struggle to move on from listening to the story to focusing on the issues.

Making an initial assessment

As the client is telling the story as she sees it, the adviser is using active listening skills and assessing what appear to be the key issues. The adviser will check these with the client by paraphrasing and summarising. At this point the adviser is also recording internally those beliefs and attitudes of the client which may have to be challenged at a later stage in the interview process. It is not usually necessary for the adviser to make notes during the interview. This can damage the cooperative relationship, as the client may become deflected by such confused thoughts as 'Why is he writing that bit down?' and may begin to select more carefully what she contributes, thus losing the spontaneity of the session.

An integral part of the initial assessment is determining the client's level of vocational maturity.[2] The four elements to be explored are:

- the extent and depth of the client's self-knowledge;
- the source and accuracy of her job knowledge;
- the extent of her decision-making skills;

- the level of development of her transition skills in applying and being interviewed for jobs or courses.

The theme of working with clients at different levels of vocational maturity is expanded in Chapter 6.

The adviser's assessment of these elements facilitates the clarification of issues which require exploration. At this point, inconsistencies in what the client is saying, doing or believing may become apparent. The adviser's task in the clarifying phase is to record these internally in order to challenge and, it is hoped, resolve them at a later stage.

THE EXPLORING PHASE

The tasks in the exploring phase are:

- building the contract;
- exploring the issues within the contract;
- encouraging the client to explore other options;
- re-examining the contract.

Building the contract

All interviews are of necessity limited in time – whether they last five minutes, or an hour, or comprise a series of meetings. In order to use effectively whatever time is available, there must be an agreement at an early stage of what can be realistically achieved in that time. Clients' expectations vary. It is essential that the adviser clarifies these and identifies the key issues and priorities. It may be clear that there are too many issues to work on in the time available, or it may emerge that the most important issue is not the one which was originally expressed by the client.

The advantage of having a contract in place is that both client and adviser are clear about their expectations of each other. When a client tends to ramble or go off in a variety of directions, or seems to be avoiding the issue, the adviser has a structure which can be used to bring the client back to effective working.

Getting to this stage in the interview model can take a very short time or it can take up a considerable proportion of the interview. It must be dictated by the pace at which the client is prepared to move and must never be rushed. The relationship which has developed – of listening, understanding, trust and working together – is the one on which the rest of the interview will be based.

Summarising is a key skill in contract forming. It helps the client to see where and how the interview is progressing and maintains the spirit of working together.

The client must make the contract her own, taking responsibility for what has been agreed. The adviser should be quite specific in spelling out the agreement and what will be worked on over the time of the interview. The adviser's clarification of the issues and precision of language at this point provide a sound model for the client and will encourage her to be specific.

The contract, however, may need to be changed during the interview. Sometimes a key issue will not emerge until well on in the process. The client may wait until the empathy is strong and the trust and understanding are firmly in place before disclosing a core difficulty. In this instance the adviser may want to renegotiate the contract. For example:

Adviser: We agreed a while ago that we should use the time we have to explore what is important to you in a job. You've just been talking though about how angry you feel at your father for pushing you into this course. Perhaps you would like to concentrate on that for a bit?

or

Adviser: You say you want to work on completing this application form. But we've seen that you are not really sure whether this is the kind of work you want to do. Perhaps we need to concentrate on that today.

Some advisers may be concerned that in the second case the issue of the application form will not be dealt with. We would argue that time spent on an application form without working on the more crucial issue is likely to be time wasted for both the adviser and the client. The client will be in a much better position to complete it if the key issue has been addressed. The issue of the application form can always be picked up again at the action-planning stage. There may be more than one way to deal with the application form – the client could be encouraged to return with a first draft, the adviser could make comments by post or another appointment could be made.

For instance, this client is beginning to face up to redundancy and to consider future options:

Candy: It's all so confusing. I've got very mixed feelings about leaving the company – I suppose I've been here far too long. I have been feeling stale for some time but just couldn't be bothered to do anything about it. I want to see this as a new opportunity, but the market's a difficult place out there. I don't know what I could do. Perhaps this is the time to start having a family. My husband is certainly keen, but it seems so weak to get pregnant just because I've been made redundant.

Adviser: It's not surprising you're feeling confused. There seem to be a lot of issues around. Perhaps we could just summarise what they are.

- You feel being made redundant has forced you to look at what you want for the next phase of your life.
- You're worried about facing the job market and feel it is time you stretched yourself again.
- One option is to have a baby, but you're concerned that you would do so as the easy way out.
- You're not sure which options are available related to your experience.

Candy: Yes, that just about sums it up.
Adviser: The issues are obviously interlinked. Our time today is limited. Perhaps we could consider just one issue in depth at the moment, and then review where we are.
Candy: I'd like to explore what my recent experience could lead to.

This summary demonstrates that the adviser understands the complexity of what the client is experiencing and moves towards making a contract on what it is feasible to work on at this point. The client is actively involved in the forming of the contract and in recognising reality.

Renegotiating the contract at any point in the interview involves the adviser inserting into the process a 'micro' version of the model. There is a need in all of the above instances to *clarify* the issue which has emerged; to *explore* its relevance, and its importance at this time; to *evaluate* its priority; and to *plan the action* to deal with it within the interview process.

Exploring the issues within the contract

Once the client has agreed which issues are appropriate to work on with the adviser in this interview, the adviser can begin to explore these in depth. The process of examining the level of vocational maturity of the client aids this exploration. The questions the adviser is asking himself internally include:

- How and why has this issue become important at this time?
- How well has the client linked what she knows about herself with what she knows about the issue?
- What are the inconsistencies?
- What gaps in knowledge are there?

The adviser will draw on skills of active listening, paraphrasing, summarising and some skilful questioning to help the client examine the issue in more depth.

Encouraging the client to explore other options

There are two possible objectives at this stage. First, by broadening the range of options being explored, the client may develop greater insight into what is important. For example:

Adviser: You've been talking about entering the advertising world because you want to be in a creative environment. There are other jobs which involve that sort of environment. Would you like to tell me to what extent you have explored these?

David: Well, I've not really looked at anything else very closely. A creative environment . . . [Pauses for reflection.] . . . I suppose there are areas like the theatre or art galleries, and I expect you would have to be creative with primary teaching. But none of these offers the excitement I see in advertising.

Adviser: Excitement?

David: Yes. It's the contact with the clients that appeals to me. Persuading them to buy my ideas.

Adviser: So it's not just a creative environment you are looking for, but also the commercial context?

David: Yes, that's right.

Second, it may become clear to the adviser at an early stage that the options under consideration are not appropriate as a consequence of the client's inability to meet the selection requirements or likely lack of success in a highly competitive market. For instance:

Adviser: We've been exploring how you might train as a PE teacher. As you've just said, there is no guarantee you will get on a course because it is so competitive. Do you think it would be sensible to look at other areas where you could develop your interest in sport just in case it doesn't work out?

Evelyn: Yes, but I have no idea what else there is.

At this point the adviser can suggest some possibilities to help the client move on, but the adviser must be wary of launching into a monologue to impart all the information available. The client is exploring ideas at this stage. The purpose is to broaden the client's perspective and by doing so to let the client become more aware of what key factors are important to her in a job. The adviser may flag the possibilities of further reading or computer-aided guidance systems to gain further ideas (see Chapter 9).

Re-examining the contract

This task may be completed internally by the adviser. If it seems appropriate to continue to work with these options in the time available, the adviser will proceed to the evaluation phase. On the other hand, this method of exploring the options may have enabled the client to raise other more deep-seated, personal issues to work with and the adviser may decide to offer the client the opportunity to redefine the contract. This opportunity in itself affirms the person-centred nature of the process and will help the client to realise the importance of addressing the other issues. Where the client has drifted away from the contract, or lost focus, this re-examination of the contract will help both the adviser and the client to reassess where they are.

For instance, this client has been unable to find a job using the nursing qualification she has just completed. She wants to explore other options but keeps mentioning, with some hesitation, a vacation job she did some years ago.

Adviser: We agreed earlier on that we would discuss options other than those related to nursing. I've noticed that

every time we try to explore which tasks you might
enjoy and be good at, you return to the job in the pub
where you were given a lot of responsibility. It sounds
as if there is something there which is holding you
back from exploring other jobs. Perhaps we should
spend some time talking about that experience.

Fiona   It's difficult to talk about. I don't know if I just made
[hesitantly]: a mess of it or they asked too much of me. I'm scared
to find myself in that position again. It's true – it
really has left its mark on my self-confidence.

THE EVALUATING PHASE

- challenging inconsistencies;
- enabling the client to weigh up the pros and cons for each option;
- prioritising options with the client;
- re-examining the contract.

Challenging inconsistencies

It is at this point in the interview that the adviser will begin to
draw attention to the connections she has made between what
the client says, does and believes at various times in the interview. The higher-level skills of challenging, judicious information
provision, immediacy and self-disclosure will be employed to help
the client view his circumstances in a more realistic way. This is
a particularly important task in the interview process, and one of
the most effective if done skilfully. It is also one of the most
difficult tasks to master and often involves some discomfort. If
the task is neglected, the client's ability to gain new insights about
self is severely limited. If, however, this task is faced it can mark
a real turning point in the interview and can enable the client to
see his world in new, more realistic and ultimately more rewarding
ways. Challenging inconsistencies and other higher-level skills are
explored in detail in Chapter 6.

Enabling the client to weigh up the pros and cons for
each option

Throughout the evaluating phase, the adviser is beginning to
lay the groundwork for the action-planning phase. As the client

explores the features of each option he will become aware of gaps in his knowledge which may limit his ability to evaluate the options. The adviser can employ a number of strategies to aid evaluation, which will be described in Chapter 6. For each option there is a need to clarify the factors involved, and to explore and evaluate them before taking action to decide on the appropriateness of that option.

Prioritising options with the client

With increased self-awareness and insights into self in relation to jobs, the client is able to begin to move towards making decisions about which options are the most appropriate to follow up. It is important to note that this list of priorities need not be a list of job titles. Depending on the circumstances, it could be the degree to which the individual factors are important to the client and the order of their importance; e.g. 'live in Scotland, job with training, involvement with the public, working in a team ...' – or it could be the prioritising of issues which will have to be addressed before career decisions can be effected; e.g. 'the difficult relationship with my boss, the opportunities for training ...'.

Re-examining the contract

As with the exploring phase, this gives the adviser the opportunity to check internally, but also externally with the client if necessary, that the interview is following the agreed course. It is always possible that the client will wait until this stage, far on in the interview, to reveal a real concern. For example:

Adviser: So far we've been through your CV and decided on some changes, but I sense there is something else concerning you.

Gordon: It's hard to get the words out. Do you think it will matter ... do employers get put off by ... Well, I'm concerned that I will be rejected because I'm so obviously gay.

Adviser: It sounds as if you are really worried about how being gay will affect how employers see you. Would you like to spend some of our time exploring this a bit more?

It may be that the issue which emerges at this time or even later in the interview is so great, of such complexity or sensitivity to the client that the adviser decides the time left is not enough to deal with it adequately. The adviser can feel a sense of frustration or irritation that this has emerged now. The issue may, however, have been in the client's awareness all the time, influencing how he has communicated. It may only be at this point that he feels secure enough to reveal it. It is vital that it is acknowledged as an important issue. How the adviser deals with it depends on the nature of the issue, the circumstances of the interview and its setting (e.g. if there is privacy, if more time is available) and the level of expertise and confidence of the adviser.

THE ACTION PLANNING PHASE

The tasks in the action-planning phase are:

- helping the client to identify what needs to be done;
- encouraging the client to formulate an appropriate systematic plan of action;
- introducing the concept of referral, if necessary;
- reviewing the contract;
- ending the interview.

Helping the client to identify what needs to be done

To be able to continue to work on the process by herself, the client needs help to clarify her understanding of the process and what she still needs to do. The careers adviser has a range of tools which will help in this part of the process. They include:

- written careers information and databases;
- pencil and paper exercises (e.g. in self-assessment workbooks);
- card sorts (e.g. identifying skills acquired in work experience by arranging individual skill cards in appropriate order);
- computer-aided guidance systems;
- psychometric tests and questionnaires;
- practice interviews (sometimes using video equipment);
- short experience courses;
- work-shadowing;
- local contacts.

The careers adviser will use his professional skills to determine which of these tools might be most effective in enabling this particular client to take the process forward. Obviously there is a need to be selective, and the client must be encouraged to take part in this process of selection. From her own experiences the client may know what is likely to be most effective according to her preferred learning style. Too many suggested actions from the adviser will only lead to confusion for the client.

Encouraging the client to formulate an appropriate systematic plan of action

In this context there is a number of basic principles:

1 The client must own the action plan. She must be involved in its development, in deciding which specific actions are appropriate in what timescale. Once the issue has been identified as worthy of development, the adviser *clarifies* what this means for the client, helps her to *explore* suitable approaches, to *evaluate* each approach and to *make the decision* on how and when to proceed.
2 Each task in the action plan must be within the reach of the client. If the tasks agreed are too numerous or too complex, the client will become demotivated and unable to complete the list of tasks. The adviser assists the client to break major tasks down into smaller, more achievable action points, so that progress can be achieved and observed, and confidence gained.
3 The action plan takes account of the client's ability to operate independently. It is easy for a client who has made progress during an interview to be carried away with enthusiasm to continue the process. The adviser must use his judgement to maintain the appropriate balance between what he knows the client needs to do and what the client feels able to do.
4 The action plan must also suit the pace at which the client works, taking account of other influences on the time available to the client.
5 The client must be encouraged to consider what might hold her back from working through the action plan and to identify who or what could help her to overcome this.

Introducing the concept of referral, if necessary

We have discussed this in more detail in Chapter 2. This is, however, part of identifying what needs to be done and of developing the action plan. We deal with it here as a separate item, as many advisers lack confidence in making a referral when sensing that the client could usefully see a counsellor to work through a personal issue which may or may not be immediately obviously career-related. Careers advisers make all sorts of referrals all the time – to see an employer or to visit a local contact. Why, then, do advisers tend to find these specific referrals difficult? It may be because personal referrals require greater skills:

1 If an adviser has offered a safe framework and an empathic approach, then the client will begin to trust. If the trust has then enabled the client to be more in touch with painful personal issues which in some way, however apparently obscure, relate to that person's development, then it is important for the adviser to be confident, clear and understanding.
2 The paramount skill at this point is for the adviser to listen without fear, knowing that tears are a release and often a relief. Tears are a natural human response to pain, and if the adviser's sense of that naturalness can be conveyed through a calm and confident listening then the meaning of the distress will emerge and the advisability of a referral to a trained counsellor will become clearer.

It is the adviser's responsibility only to give the client the opportunity and the means through referral to explore these issues. The client then decides whether to follow through or not.

3 The client may become emotional (angry or distressed) at the suggestion and the adviser may be afraid of not being able to handle the feelings. As mentioned above, it may, ultimately, be useful if a client bursts into tears. Once again the empathy which has already been developed acts as a cushion and enables the client to feel safe. Sometimes the outpouring of emotions is exactly what a client needs in order to be able to gain some insights into what is going on.

Whatever the referral, it is vital that the adviser has trust in the professionalism of the person to whom the referral is made. This entails the adviser developing a network of appropriate contacts over a period of time. The client will usually decide whether to refer herself or have the adviser make the first contact. Self-referral is always preferable, as the client takes more responsibility and is therefore more likely to be motivated to keep the referral appointment. Some clients, however, prefer the adviser to make the contact. Before any information is passed on to the personal counsellor, it must always be discussed with the client. There may be elements of her story which she does not wish to be revealed until she has developed a trusting relationship with the other counsellor. It is probably best to telephone in the presence of the client so that she knows precisely what has been communicated.

Reviewing the contract

Towards the end of the interview the adviser should refer back to the contract, spelling out the issues which were to be worked on and reviewing progress so far. This encourages the client to recognise how much progress has been made and to be aware of the other issues which may still need to be resolved, either within that session or as 'homework'.

Ending the interview

Clients who have been listened to and have become involved in the process often want to continue beyond the time allotted and resist the ending of the session. Sometimes, on the point of departure, a client suddenly produces a key issue which will clearly take some considerable time to explore. The adviser who has effectively set the parameters for the interview right at the beginning and established a working contract can afford to be firm with the client. How the situation is handled does depend on the nature of the issue. The client may simply wish to prolong the time with the adviser, or may have found a key issue emerging as the end approaches. Either way, it is important to stick to the contracted time. Initially, advisers often struggle to learn the assertiveness required to end an interview gently and finally. Yet it is an extremely important skill, for what is communicated through a firm and positive ending is a sense of the adviser's belief in the client's capacity to manage on her own. This is usually a good way of building the client's confidence. For instance:

Adviser: Well, you've brought up another big issue there. As we mentioned when we started, our time today is limited and it is drawing to an end. Perhaps we could arrange to meet another time to discuss this issue.

On the other hand, the client may have deliberately held back with this issue as it is potentially so painful to bring into the open. It is only when she sees the opportunity to raise it beginning to slip away that she forces herself to produce it. The adviser has an important decision to make but, whatever the decision, the vital element of the adviser's strategy at this point must be the acknowledgement of the importance of the issue for the client. For example:

Adviser: I can see it was very difficult for you to mention your difficulties with your boss just now. You are quite right – it must be having an effect on your self-confidence. You know our time is nearly finished today, but if you want to talk through what is happening at work we can arrange another appointment, although it may not be soon.

For some advisers, it is impossible in the work setting to see this client again. This may require referral to another colleague or another professional.

Endings can be painful. Where the relationship which has developed has been effective in moving the client on, and where some painful feelings have been expressed, there is a sense of loss on the part of both the client and the adviser. To enable an effective transition the adviser should review with the client what has happened, summarising the key points discussed and the decisions made about actions to be taken. A useful strategy is to encourage the client to summarise for herself what she perceives has happened. The purpose of the summary is fourfold:

- to help the client 'own' what has happened and provide an overview of the progress which has been made;
- to check that the client's perceptions are accurate;
- to enable the client to begin to move out of the relationship in order to work independently;
- to allow any strong feelings which have emerged to subside – for example, the client who has been distressed may value the opportunity to be quietly on her own for a little while.

At the end of this chapter it is hoped the reader will have a sense that this model is dynamic. The shape of the model is constantly changing according to the emerging issues and the needs of each client. The adviser using such a model has a structure on which to base counselling skills and assess progress. A micro version of the model can be utilised within the interview. By working with the client in such a structured manner the adviser is demonstrating a methodology which the perceptive and receptive client can adopt when working alone. As we mentioned at the beginning of this chapter, the model is only a model. It must be underpinned by the skills and orientation of counselling which will enable the adviser to move the client effectively through the process of the model. These skills are described in the following chapter.

Chapter 5

Counselling skills

As outlined in Chapter 2, the essential links between all forms of counselling relationships are the core skills which underpin any effective communication model. Those using counselling skills in careers advisory, nursing or bereavement work share these core skills, whether this means therapeutic counselling or information provision, in a contracted series of sessions or within an hour or during a brief discussion. The skills are fundamental in establishing the essential trust in the relationship, clarifying issues of importance to the client and beginning to work on these issues to a point where the client can take continued action independently.

There are many descriptions of the core skills in a counselling setting. Particularly useful examples for the careers context are to be found in Sue Culley's *Integrative Counselling Skills in Action* and Gerard Egan's *The Skilled Helper*.[1] In this chapter we shall illustrate the skills with specific examples drawn from the careers context in relation to the model described in the previous chapter. Certain skills are more basic or fundamental than others, and we have therefore grouped the range of counselling skills on three levels. All are essential in an effective helping relationship but cannot operate independently. Figure 5.1 offers a simple way of understanding this inter-relationship of different skills. We shall first outline the skills of the pyramid in this figure before going into more practical detail about each set of skills.

At the base of the pyramid are the fundamental skills of listening to the client in every sense – *actively listening* to:

- the content of what is being said;
- how it is said;

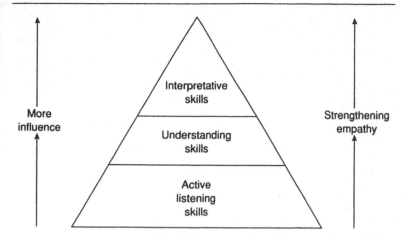

Figure 5.1 The skills pyramid

- the possible meaning behind the words;
- the feeling expressed;
- the nature of the silences which occur.

It also involves actively listening to what is happening to the adviser in response to what is said and assessing the feelings which are aroused by this client. The listening lays down the framework for empathy, without which the adviser cannot begin to use any of the other levels of skills in the pyramid.

The next level includes the *understanding* skills of restating, paraphrasing, summarising, some forms of questioning and encouraging the client to move forward. These skills are referred to as reflective or responding skills. The empathy which has been established early in the interview continues to develop as the client is encouraged to review what is said, to examine it and to begin to understand it.

The power of feeling understood by another cannot be over-estimated. It can be overwhelming and sometimes produces a sudden rush of unexpected emotion. Whenever these skills are employed it is essential that the fundamental listening skills are in place – the second level cannot operate effectively without the first.

The previous chapter described how the model allows the adviser to manage the general shape of the interview while still enabling the client to do his own exploring. The counselling skills themselves are an integral part of both managing and enabling to varying degrees.

The skills at the next level of the pyramid allow the counsellor greater influence in what is happening. The fundamental listening skills involve the least influence, but the adviser is still exercising some element of direction by making appropriate minimal encouraging responses and displaying relevant body language at appropriate points in the interview. At the next level, with the understanding skills, this influence is more evident – what and how the adviser paraphrases, summarises and questions has a bearing on the direction and level of depth which the interview achieves.

The final group of skills at the top of the pyramid includes the various skills of challenging immediacy, disclosure and information giving. We call them *interpretative* skills, as it is here the adviser is conveying her interpretation of the issues involved for the client. These higher-level skills give the adviser a great deal of influence in selecting specific areas to explore with the client and neglecting others for the time being. To be able to use these, a strong level of empathy must have already developed. The adviser must maintain and develop that empathy by continuing to employ listening and understanding skills. As the exchange moves through the process as described in the model, the adviser uses the fundamental listening skills during the entire interview, introducing the understanding skills at an early point in the clarifying stage, but does not start to use the interpretative skills until the exploring stage at the earliest.

Summarising these points, it is clear that:

- none of the levels of skills will stand alone;
- the higher up the pyramid, the greater the level of influence of the adviser;
- at the higher level the adviser builds on the strength of the empathy developed through the skills at the base of the pyramid;
- the effectiveness of the helping relationship is dependent on the adviser's facility with the skills at all levels.

All of these skills will be explored in detail below and illustrated with examples drawn from the careers context in the next section of this chapter. Chapter 10 provides a demonstration of how these skills are integrated into the practice of a career advisory relationship with an actual client.

ACTIVE LISTENING SKILLS

Active listening skills are complex, operating at many levels of awareness and using the adviser's eyes, ears and awareness of personal feelings in order to determine what the client is really trying to say. Active listening is fundamental to the establishment of basic empathy. It demonstrates the essential nature of the helping relationship, namely that the client's words and beliefs are important and valued by the counsellor. Unless the adviser actively listens, the client will not develop the trust to believe that this could be a helping relationship. An adviser who does not do this is likely to miss insights into the true nature of the issues concerning the client.

Observing the client's behaviour

The first element of active listening involves observing the client's behaviour. What she does and how she tells her story convey important messages from the very first contact. The adviser notes the body language, the level of eye contact, the tone of voice, any hesitancy in talking about the issues. An internal dialogue helps the adviser to record and begin to think about the possible meaning of these messages.

In the first stages of the interview the adviser might make the following observations:

- 'She seems very bright and cheerful, is talking very quickly and smiling a lot. But there is very little eye contact – in fact she is refusing to catch my eye. I wonder if something is making her very anxious about this interview?'

or

- 'He moved his chair away a bit when he sat down and is sitting sideways on it. He is clearly struggling to get the words out and they all appear to end in a question mark. He seems to be seeking reassurance from me all the time. I wonder if he has a general lack of confidence or if he is just uncomfortable in this interview situation?'

Later in the interview the adviser's inner reflections might be as follows:

- 'Whenever she talks about her year teaching abroad she fiddles with her rings and slows her speech down. She also keeps returning to that period in her life – perhaps something happened then which has a strong bearing on how she sees the future.'

Listening to the client's words

The next element of active listening involves attending to the implications of what the client is saying. The adviser needs to understand how the client perceives her situation, what are the important values which seem to govern her perceptions and the level of her ability to relate these self-perceptions to the world outside. For instance:

Susan: I thought of social work. I'd like to help people. I don't like the idea of the profit motive, so it will have to be the public sector. Anyway I'm better in the background than at the sharp end.

Adviser's internal dialogue: She doesn't seem to have much understanding of the nature of the public sector today. I wonder what she understands by 'helping others' and 'profit motive'?

Listening to the adviser's feelings

The next element in active listening involves the adviser's own feelings about what is happening in the exchange. These may be of two kinds. The first are those feelings which give clues about what is happening for the client; e.g. where the adviser is experiencing a heavy sense of despair or sudden anger which is unexplained, the feelings may have been picked up from the client. We will explore how to work with this when we look at the skill of immediacy.

In this example, an adviser is interviewing a discontinuing student who is discussing her initial reasons for choosing her course. As she talks about her parents' involvement, the counsellor begins to feel intensely angry:

Adviser's internal dialogue: This anger must be from the client. Although she is not voicing it, I wonder if she is angry because she feels she was pushed into this course and blames her parents for the situation she is now in?

The second kind of feelings which the adviser must listen to are those emerging from his own value systems or experiences. For example, the adviser may notice strong feelings, such as intensely liking or disliking something, or of strongly identifying with something, or he may notice that working with a particular client strikes a chord that evokes feelings which can hamper an effective helping relationship. Where an issue for the client is one that has been recently experienced by the adviser, but not yet fully dealt with, the adviser may not be able to separate his own personal feelings from those of the client; for example, if the adviser has been recently bereaved. In such instances where the adviser can find himself very closely identifying with the client in a way that seems to detract from the relationship, it may be appropriate to refer the client to another adviser.

Listening to silence

At an early stage in the development of expertise, advisers may find difficulty in allowing silences to happen. If the adviser still bears the responsibility for producing the 'right' answers, there is strong motivation to break a silence and move the client on. There might be an assumption that nothing is happening when no words are said. There are in reality many things which could be happening in the silence:

- the client may be reviewing what has already been said;
- the client may have just realised something very important as a result of a comment from the adviser and may need time to absorb its meaning;
- the client may be deciding just how much it is safe to reveal;
- the client may be experiencing some strong emotion which is too painful to put into words just yet.

Wherever possible, the client should be allowed to break the silence for herself. The adviser's role is not to intervene, but to be there for the client when she is ready. The adviser can help best by sitting quietly, conveying with an open body language his readiness to resume the discussion whenever the client is able. Fiddling with papers, writing notes and other distractions are a reflection of the adviser's discomfort and are intrusive on the client's thoughts.

When to break a silence

When the client shows discomfort with the silence, a simple comment is appropriate to offer support. For example, 'Just take your time. I'm here when you're ready', may encourage a client to stay with her silence if it is appropriate.

When the counsellor senses that the silence has gone on in a way that seems uncomfortable for both, it may be that the client is not able to resolve the dilemma of how much to reveal. The counsellor can respond by acknowledging there may be a problem; for example:

Adviser: I guess this topic seems difficult and perhaps you are not sure I will be able to understand.

or

Adviser: Sometimes it is difficult to find a starting point when it all feels so confused.

When is a silence too long? This is indefinable. It depends on:

- the circumstances of the interview. Is it in a public office or somewhere private?;
- the client. Some individuals find silence very uncomfortable and unproductive;
- the adviser's level of competence. Experience will enable the adviser to allow a client to be silent in a productive way;
- whether the adviser suspects his responses have disturbed a client who may be feeling a strong sense of anger or sadness and has deliberately withdrawn from the interview. This can happen even with the most experienced advisers, but is least likely to be the case where the empathy is strong and the adviser allows the client to move on at her own pace. A reluctance to continue with the exchange is destructive and should be addressed sooner rather than later. For instance:

Adviser [In   I'm getting the sense that you didn't like what I said
an inviting   just now. Perhaps we could talk about how you feel
tone]:   about it.

Listening – what the client hears

The client is also listening to what the counsellor is communicating through words, body language and tone of voice. Some of this listening is done consciously, but the client picks up much of it at a subconscious level. What the client picks up will influence how she sees her role in the process and how the empathy can develop. Consider these two scenarios:

1 The adviser sits, pen poised ready to take notes, occasionally glancing at the client as she tells her story. The client falters as the notes are taken but is encouraged to continue when the counsellor looks up expectantly.

   The client's internal dialogue could be: 'I wonder what he is going to write down? I'd better not get it wrong. Maybe I shouldn't tell him too much. Why did he write that bit down? What will he make of all this?' The client's level of anxiety is raised.

2 The adviser sits slightly leaning forward, hands relaxed in his lap. As the client tells the story he nods encouragingly, sometimes smiling at what is said, occasionally offering minimal encouragers – 'Hm, hm', etc.

   This client's internal dialogue could be 'He doesn't seem over-anxious about all this. He seems friendly and it looked as if he is really listening to me. He didn't look shocked when I told him I'd been sacked. Maybe he will understand my side of the story.'

Throughout the interview, the adviser is listening to the facts of what the client says or does, assessing their accuracy and what clues are provided about the client's perceptions of the issues. Active listening involves attending at a deeper level to the feelings conveyed by the client and those generated within the adviser. It is clearly a complex set of skills. Not only is the adviser trying to attend to what the client says, the tone of voice used, the body language, but at the same time he is trying to record and analyse internally what is happening both for himself and in response to the client. The adviser is also formulating the next response to encourage the client to move forward. Throughout all this the adviser is conveying a caring, trusting, open attitude.

UNDERSTANDING SKILLS

It is all very well to surmise internally what the client may be meaning, but the interview cannot progress until the adviser has checked out her understanding with the client. This group of skills facilitates the growth of trust and honesty, and enables the client to confirm or correct what the adviser has understood. They are the basis for beginning to acquire new insights into what is important.

These skills are restating, paraphrasing, summarising and questioning. Their use can achieve a number of objectives:

- to demonstrate that the adviser is actively listening to what is being said;
- to convey the essential qualities of caring and understanding;
- to check out the reality of the adviser's understanding;
- to encourage the client to move on.

Restating

Restating is a very simple and effective way of conveying active listening. It can involve repeating just one word to help the client to focus on a particular issue, or can mean the repetition of a whole phrase or sentence. The adviser selects with care what she restates, picking up a word or phrase which seems crucial in what the client is saying.

This client, for instance, is a married woman returning to the world of work after some time at home looking after her family:

Mandy: I'm not sure why I'm here. I really feel very apprehensive about going back to work.

Adviser: Apprehensive?

Mandy: Yes. Ambivalent really. I want to do the right thing for the children, but I really need to get out of the house and be with grown-up people.

In this case, a student is discussing her performance at a job interview where the adviser suspects she might have come across as aggressive:

Sophie: I don't know why they rejected me. After all, I went out of my way to demonstrate my skills of critical analysis.

Adviser: Demonstrate your skills of critical analysis?'

Sophie: Yes. I told them what is wrong with their image and how useless their brochure is. Well, I suppose it's possible I wasn't very tactful.

Restating enables the adviser to encourage clients to reflect on the meaning of what they are saying, thereby increasing their understanding. Using the client's own words conveys the fact that the adviser is listening, without judgement. Restating is an effective skill which can be quickly learned and put into practice. The danger lies in overuse. The client comes to expect it and sees it as a technique being employed and therefore as mechanical or artificial. It can then undermine the development of empathy. The client begins to choose words carefully and this will inhibit real communication.

Paraphrasing

Paraphrasing uses the adviser's words to reflect the gist of what the client has said. Using the adviser's words helps to convince the client that the adviser is listening. It can be particularly useful where the client has struggled to tell the story or is confused about the issues. The client can see more clearly what he is trying to say, focus on the key issues, and begin to move to a deeper level where he can identify and express feelings about what is going on.

This client is describing her perceptions of teaching as a career after work-shadowing in her own old secondary school. She is now unsure if teaching is for her.

Mary: It was a bit strange – I got on really well with the kids; they were very chatty. The teacher (he had taught me) was very encouraging, I suppose. He even let me teach a lesson, but I was very uncomfortable about it.

Adviser: It sounds as if you were uncomfortable about teaching in front of your ex-teacher.

Mary: Yes. And I was always a bit in awe of that teacher. He kept impressing on me how hard he has to work. Then he started to push me to work with the sixth-year class every week. I wanted to help, but this is my final year and I have my dissertation to complete.

Adviser: So you feel pressurised by this teacher to take on some work you do not really have time for?

Mary: That's right. Then he began to imply that I would never get on a teacher training course if I did not help out. I did not plan to get so involved at this point, you know. I have other ideas I want to check out. I just wanted to get a flavour of what the job is all about.

Adviser [Reflecting feeling]: You sound angry when you say that.

Mary: Yes. Angry and used. Perhaps it was a mistake to go back to my old school. I might get a clearer picture if I try a different school.

Through paraphrasing and reflecting feeling, the counsellor enables the client to clarify what it is about the experience that has coloured her view of teaching. The client feels understood; she is enabled to express her feelings, and to begin to recognise her more 'adult' role as teacher and the difficulty of trying out that role in a place where she still *felt* like a pupil.

Summarising

Summarising, like paraphrasing, is a skill which provides an opportunity to check out the adviser's perceptions and is used most effectively at key points in the interview to clarify what has been said at points where there is a need to move on – e.g. from evaluating to action planning. Where several issues emerge, summarising can help the client focus on what is most important at the time and to prioritise the others. It is particularly useful at the point of forming a contract. An effective summary ensures that the client feels understood and that the most important things are being heard, but he also becomes aware that some issues may be more appropriately dealt with in another setting or at another time.

In this example, the client is a potential mature student discussing the choice of his course. After about ten minutes the adviser attempts to summarise her perceptions of the client's main concerns as follows:

Adviser: It seems you have a number of concerns about starting a course at college:

- You're worried about funding if you give up your part-time job.
- You're afraid you might not fit in with other students.

- You are anxious about whether you will cope academically.
- You are concerned that the course which interests you might not lead to a job.

That's a lot for us to explore – perhaps you could say what you would like to look at today?

Mike: I really do want an interesting job. Once I find somewhere to live I'll be able to concentrate on that. (I slept on a friend's floor last night.) It would be wonderful to be able to make use of my experience in the theatre, but since I fell out with my parents I've had money worries and my student loan will have to be paid off. A good job with prospects – that's what we all want, isn't it? Perhaps if I find a flat I can get some more box office experience. I know I will need further training.

Adviser: What I seem to be hearing is that you have a strong interest in work in the theatre, but it is hard to concentrate on possible job areas in the future when you do have these money worries.

Mike: Oh yes. That's on my mind all the time.

At the end of the exploration stage of our model, the adviser might summarise the issues which have been explored with the intention of beginning to move into the evaluation stage. Or, having worked through the evaluation stage the adviser might summarise what has been said so far by the client in preparation for identifying the actions the client will require to take in order to continue the process. For instance:

Adviser: Could we try to recap for a moment? We've talked about some of the options which would enable you to use your interest in art. You feel that your ability does not match your interests, so you're not sure about taking a further course in art. You would, however, like to work in an artistic environment and you are prepared to take some training which would help you get started. Is that the way you see it?

Sometimes the adviser will struggle to understand her client and it is important to remember that our perceptions may be coloured by our own experiences, by our culture and values, or by our previous contacts with clients in similar situations. To achieve empathy we have to be able to see as clearly as possible in the way the client sees the world. Paraphrasing and summarising are never offered as a statement of fact, but as part of a process of understanding. Even if our understanding is not accurate, so long as it is presented in a gentle, tentative manner, it can provide the opportunity for the client to ponder further, correct the mistake and take a collaborative part in thinking about the process. Useful starting phrases might include:

- 'You seem to be saying . . .'
- 'What I think I'm hearing . . .'
- 'I think you may be feeling . . .'
- 'Could we try to clarify at this point what it is you are saying?'
- 'Let me try to summarise what you are saying.'

Questioning

There is a variety of questioning styles, some of which can be used effectively and others which inhibit the client's active involvement in the process of the interview. A barrage of questions takes the responsibility away from the client, can be extremely threatening and will result in the client reducing participation in communication.

More effective questions are 'open', that is they do not imply a correct or expected answer or encourage a minimal response (yes/no); e.g. 'What thoughts have you been having about . . .?', 'Can you tell me more about . . .?', 'Which particular aspects of social work make you apprehensive?' Their objectives are:

- to offer the opportunity to expand on what has been said;
- to encourage the client to provide additional relevant information;
- to clarify what the client is saying;
- to encourage the client to be specific in what is said;
- to help the client to move on.

Questions should be based on what the client has already said – often a paraphrase or a summary. A question outside the client's framework can easily devalue what he has already said. He might then feel he had somehow got it wrong, becoming confused about the purpose of the question and reluctant to respond effectively to the question. An effective question starts within the client's framework. For instance:

Adviser: So you have an interest in training as a chartered accountant. Can you tell me what sort of things you have been doing to find out about the work?

This direct question seeks information which will help the adviser to assess the client's level of vocational maturity, to identify needs and to encourage the client to be specific. Another example is:

Adviser: You say you've just heard about your exam results. They do show that your marks are much lower than expected. Could you tell me a bit about how you are feeling about that?

This question is asked in a tentative manner to a student who is clearly feeling bruised. It encourages the client to express potentially painful feelings without forcing the issue. Other situations may be even more difficult:

Lydia: I just don't know what to do. If I take a job abroad, I would leave my mother on her own. She has been widowed just a few months. I'm not sure any job is worth it. I haven't even had the courage to tell her about it yet. On the other hand, I'd be denying myself a tremendous opportunity – I expect she wouldn't want me to lose that.

Adviser: You sound apprehensive about how your mother will react when you tell her. How do you imagine she will be?

With this question, the adviser moves the client along in the process by encouraging her to imagine herself in the difficult situation. It may allow her to explore more fully what is holding her back from making a decision (e.g. fear of her mother dying too, or her own personal fear about tackling a new culture on her own).

Many effective open questions are introduced by the words, 'how' or 'what'. Not only do these tend to be open in the type of response which emerges, but they are also free of any form of judgement. For instance:

- 'How do you feel about moving away from home?'
- 'What factors will influence your decision?'

The word 'why', on the other hand, introduces questions which can be loaded with judgement, such as:

● 'Why are you turning down this job offer?'

'Why' questions are more threatening and may encourage the client to become defensive, or to produce the 'right' expected answer. The well-intentioned adviser may genuinely believe the 'why' question is the way to get to the heart of the matter, but it can seem too direct and force the client to move too quickly or to back off. The interview should progress at a pace which the client can manage. A combination of paraphrases, statements and sparingly used questions carries the interview along gently at the level and pace suitable for the client and offers the client a certain measure of control over what is happening.

In a desire to get to the heart of the issues it is possible to fall into the trap of asking several questions in a row without waiting for the answers. This can be as simple as a double question – either/or:

● 'Now the results are out, do you want to take the resits or do you want to change your course?'

There will be issues about either choice which need to be explored. This question is potentially confusing. An exploratory question might have been more useful – e.g. 'How do you feel right now about taking resits?' There may of course be other options which the client has in mind. In the first question, the adviser is presenting the two choices which seem valid under the circumstances, but the way the question is phrased may mean the client will reject without discussion other options which may be equally valid for him.

The following are all poor questions, and if run together invite the client to offer one-word answers and leave him uncertain about where this is leading. The client will probably feel that the adviser is taking control and wonder what she is going to do with the responses.

● 'Do you want to return to work?' (Yes/no)
● 'Do you want to go back to what you did before?' (Yes/no)
● 'What retraining are you prepared to do?' (Nothing)
● 'What arrangements have you made for the children after school?' (Nothing)

- 'Do you perhaps want to work part-time or maybe look at job sharing?' (Yes/no)

Each of these questions may have validity on their own, but where does the client begin to respond if they are all run together? – to the first question or the last? This number of questions might seem an extreme example, but it is possible to fall into just such a trap under pressure of time, especially when an inexperienced adviser is anxious to make sure all options are covered. More appropriate ways of getting to the relevant issue might include:

- 'What are the issues you feel are important to look at?'
- 'I guess you have some feelings about what you did before returning to work?'
- 'I expect you may be a bit anxious about balancing care of the children and your own work needs.'

On reading this section, it may seem that questioning holds so many inherent dangers for advisers operating a counselling approach that it should be avoided at all costs. But skilful questioning is an important part of vocational guidance, although advisers should be wary of allowing questioning to dominate the interview. An adviser's internal dialogue should clarify the purpose of posing a question and then allow it to be formulated carefully as an open question. Questions are best used in a tentative style, and in conjunction with the other skills they can be very effective. Advisers should ensure that the essential empathy is developing before asking very probing questions.

One style of question which is particularly valuable, as it is more tentative in nature, is that used in conjunction with a statement. As with other types of questioning, it can be most useful if it follows a summary or paraphrase.

This client, for example, has been talking about the circumstances leading up to his dismissal from work:

Brian: I suppose I was late a few times and I did stop going to college on day release for a while; it was so boring. They didn't like it when I told a customer she had no right to speak to me like that.

Adviser: You've mentioned a number of reasons why your employer wasn't pleased with your work. I wonder how you feel now about what happened then?

Brian: Well, I feel really sorry. I was really pleased when I got that job. So was my dad. I feel I've let everyone down.

This question seems to enable the client to take responsibility for what has gone wrong.

The skills described so far – listening, restating, paraphrasing, summarising and questioning – are essential to the creation of an empathic relationship. They are all likely to be used extensively throughout the interview but are particularly important at the beginning. They tend to generate a feeling of safety and comfort for the client. The purpose of careers counselling, however, is not just to make people feel safe and comfortable. Learning about ourselves and how we relate to the world around us can indeed be very uncomfortable, even painful. Once the basic qualities of warmth, trust and understanding are established, the adviser often needs to draw on expertise which allows exploration of the more uncomfortable issues, as these are often the ones which enable change and development to take place.

INTERPRETATIVE SKILLS

This group of skills, at the top of the pyramid in Figure 5.1, include challenging, being specific, self-disclosure and providing information. These interventions are more likely to produce insight into the way the client perceives self and the world around her. The experienced adviser will therefore make sure the empathic relationship has been developed and will then use the interpretative skills with care. Misuse of these skills can be very threatening and may be counter-productive if they are used to give power and influence to the adviser rather than the client. Used effectively, this group of skills can contribute to enhancing empathy at a much deeper level. Not all these skills are used in every interview. The adviser selects the appropriate tools to achieve the objective. The particular skill used depends on the issues involved, the level of self-awareness of the client and the relative expertise of the adviser.

Challenging

Challenging is the skill of presenting the client with the inconsistencies of what she is saying at varying levels. The inconsistency can be very obvious – e.g. the client who says she wants to work in nursing, but tells you she faints at the sight of blood. At a deeper level is the inconsistency observed in the client who seeks help in writing a CV, then never sends it to any employers.

Challenging encourages the client to bring out into the open issues which have not yet been mentioned and to gain some insight into their importance. Inconsistencies of which the client is apparently unaware may be more difficult to challenge, yet they can often give important clues about the real meaning of what the issues are and challenging them may often uncover strong emotions.

For example, a mature student talks about how supportive her husband has been while she completed her degree, but says so in a low, flat tone of voice:

Adviser: You say how supportive your husband has been. Yet when I listen to your voice it sounds as if you don't really mean it. I wonder what you are feeling about his support?

The feelings which emerge after challenging may have been deeply buried, or the client may be unaware of their existence or afraid to voice them.

Inexperienced advisers may inadvertently manage to keep a client's feelings under the surface. They may be afraid the situation will get out of control and that they will not be able to cope with the emerging feelings. Some rationalise this by saying it is an invasion of the privacy of clients to probe too deeply into their emotions. But of course emotions govern much of what we say and do, and clearly have a fundamental role in establishing how we view and react to the world around us. A client's understanding of what influences her emotions is often a strong aid to decision making and as such is a particularly legitimate area for careers advisers to explore.

Feelings as well as thoughts can help a client get a much clearer picture of her world. When a client bursts into tears, this may be exactly what is needed to enable her to begin to come to terms with an issue and move on. In one sense a client will only reveal what she really wants to reveal, and when the adviser has difficulty in coping with those particular emotions, his clients will almost certainly cover up these feelings. When the adviser can acknowledge these emotions in himself, then the client will feel safe enough to open up, and in the trust and security engendered will be able to take risks as necessary.

The extent to which it is appropriate to explore the emotional world of a client depends on:

- the time available. Where time is restricted it may be appropriate to make another appointment or refer to another adviser;
- the place. A public office or library with constant interruptions is not appropriate;
- the expertise of the adviser. It is the responsibility of the adviser to determine at what point a referral should be made. However, the skilled adviser should not jump to referral just because there are feelings involved;
- the level of self-awareness of the client. For some people the emotional world is firmly battened down. It can be extremely threatening to open it up and they may simply not be prepared to do so.

Challenging is unlikely to be used effectively in the clarifying stage of our interview model, although discrepancies in what the client is saying and/or doing can often be apparent at an early point. It is an extremely powerful tool. At its root it is active listening on all levels – what the client is saying, doing and feeling, as well as using the adviser's own reactions. It is the skill which advisers find most difficult to develop. As one trainee said, 'So I get his anger out into the open. What do I do with it then?'. One response to this could be that the expression of a strong feeling such as anger may enable the client to see where the feeling is coming from and how it is influencing (or preventing) her decision making. This can enable a better assessment of important factors and allow her to move on.

Another way of looking at this is to consider what happens if this emotion is neglected by the adviser. For example, it may be blocking the client's ability to see her own role in what is happening. A realistic assessment of how the client could react in certain circumstances in the future may be unattainable. Unexpressed feeling will cloud the recognition and evaluation of some of the options available.

It is possible that the assumptions behind the adviser's challenge are not valid, or that the perceptions may be only partially correct. Challenging must therefore be offered in a very tentative manner. Possible opening phrases include:

- 'It sounds as if . . .'
- 'I wonder if . . .'
- 'On the one hand . . . on the other . . .'
- 'I'm getting the impression that . . .'
- 'Perhaps we could look at this from another point of view.'

Examples of challenging follow.

Challenging facts

A client is discussing applying for work which requires a high level of numerical skills:

Adviser: So one of the options you want to explore is accounts work. We've learned from the job description that it would involve working with numbers and yet you mentioned before that you really struggled with your GCSE maths. I wonder if you see any difficulty there?

Another client does not make any job applications:

Adviser: You've dropped in to see me two or three times now to check out some minor changes to your CV, which is actually ready. It is interesting that you have not yet sent it off to any employers. It seems as if something is holding you back.

Challenging perceptions

A client appears to have a low self-image. She doesn't believe she has much to offer employers in the way of skills or experience:

Adviser: You say that employers will not be interested in you when the market is so competitive, yet you have done a lot of vacation work in pubs and restaurants. It seems to me that you have developed considerable expertise. If competition is frightening for you, I wonder what convinces you so firmly about this type of work?

Challenging beliefs/attitudes

A client believes recent rejections by employers have been due to racial discrimination. While not discounting this as a possibility, the adviser observes that the client appears to be increasingly aggressive in his manner as the careers interview progresses. It is the belief which is challenged, not the individual:

Adviser: Yes, it certainly is possible they were discriminating. But perhaps at this point I could share something I've observed with you as we talk. Your style is very direct, aggressive even. I'm left feeling increasingly uncomfortable. And perhaps it has the same effect when you are with an employer, and I guess this could be a contributing factor to your poor record at interviews.

Challenging feelings

In the previous example, the adviser might suspect that the aggression stems from feelings of anger derived from the perceived and/or real discrimination:

Adviser: You sound really angry when you talk about being rejected because of your colour.
Thomas: Yes. I'm very angry because it's so unfair. I do everything in the right way.
Adviser: I can certainly understand your anger – and yet I wonder if this anger from the last interview could be affecting how you behave when you have the next interview?

Being specific

An essential role of the adviser is to help the client become more specific in order to understand what she really means. Discrepancies may only appear when a client is encouraged to produce examples to demonstrate what she is saying. The adviser can encourage this in two ways.

The adviser can create the climate for the client to be specific by following the adviser's own mode of response. If from the beginning of the interview the adviser is clear and precise in what he says, the client will be encouraged to do likewise. If the client continues to make vague statements, however, the adviser will encourage her to be specific by challenging her to focus on some aspect of the statement(s). For example:

Leslie: I'd like a job with lots of variety.
Adviser   Variety?
[restating]:

In response to the student who wants 'to work with people':

Adviser: Perhaps you could tell me in what ways you see your-
            self working with people.

A student insists he wants to use his degree discipline in
employment:

Adviser: You've mentioned several times that you have enjoyed
            studying geography. Perhaps you could tell me what it
            is about the subject which interests you.

Self-disclosure

Careers advisers draw on their own life experiences – their
personal work and family circumstances, their experience of decision and crisis points. It can be very tempting to introduce these
to demonstrate understanding of what is happening with the
client, but this mode should be used very sparingly as it may divert
the focus away from the client's world. However, it is unlikely
that in the kind of careers interview we are describing it is appropriate to introduce self-disclosure. The other skills described will
nearly always be able to achieve the same goals. In certain circumstances it can be facilitative – the client gets the sense that an
adviser does understand some of her perspective, and realises that
she is not alone in having difficulty with these issues. For example:

Adviser: I remember very well how anxious I felt about my first
            job interview.

The revelation of some of the adviser's life experiences should
not be offered at an early stage and should be used sparingly once
empathy is in place.
The dangers of self-disclosure are that:

• the adviser takes control;
• the adviser could be seen to be promoting his own values;
• it may irritate clients. 'What has this to do with me?';
• it may distract the client from working on her own feelings;
• it lets the client (and the adviser) slide away from dealing with
  the client's potentially painful feelings.

It is inevitable that advisers, in their internal dialogue, relate what the client is saying to their own experiences, but the appropriateness of self-disclosure must be measured carefully. The task is to assess how self-disclosure will help the client gain new insights and to move on. The adviser's circumstances and response to them can *never* be exactly the same.

Immediacy

Immediacy is the skill of drawing the client's attention to what is happening here and now in the interview in order to enhance perspective or provide fresh insight into behaviour. It is a skill to be used very sparingly in the initial stages of the model, but if offered at an appropriate point, immediacy offers a challenge to the client in a very powerful way.

For example, a client has been discussing her poor performance at selection interviews. The adviser realises as the interview progresses that there is very little eye contact and that the client frequently interrupts:

Adviser: Perhaps I could stop you there for just a moment. I'd like to share with you something I've observed as we have been talking. I've noticed that you do not always look at me and that you sometimes interrupt me. This makes me feel as if you are perhaps not listening to what I am saying. I'm just wondering, perhaps it is possible that this is how your interviewers might be feeling?

The adviser draws attention to the observed behaviour in the session, then tentatively begins to make the connections with performance in a selection interview.

Effective provision of information

Some would argue that this is the specific skill of the careers adviser. It is what makes careers work different from most other forms of counselling.

Advisers have access to a huge body of knowledge about courses, types of work, training, employers, employment trends, etc. The skills involved include knowing when and how to offer the information to the client, knowing when the client is being swamped with information and knowing when the client is not ready to assimilate the information.

If we take at face value a request for information, the client will accept it for what it is and take it away. But what will she do with it? Unless she is able to relate that information to herself and the issues concerning her, it will not be assimilated and she is unlikely to be motivated to take action based on the information. It is certainly true that in many exchanges information is what is needed and what should be given, particularly in the shorter interviews.

Brief examples are:

- 'What do history graduates do?'
- 'What qualifications do I need to get into this course?'
- 'When do I have to apply for this job?'

There is no point in pushing the client to reveal her innermost thoughts and feelings if some simple information is all that is required. The request for information may, however, simply be the way a client decides to approach an adviser or the client may believe this is what is expected of her. The adviser must take the client from the point at which she starts. It could be that the client needs to test the adviser out – how approachable, or how judgemental is he?

The principles of providing information are:

- check out what the client already knows;
- be accurate. If an adviser does not know, it is better to suggest how the client may find out than to give inaccurate information;
- be brief. An individual can absorb only a certain amount of information at one time. Most careers information is now available in written form and on computer. The adviser can outline where and how this can be accessed. An unskilled adviser may need to demonstrate his knowledge;
- always respond to a request for information. If it is not appropriate to give it at that point, the adviser should let the client know it has not been forgotten about. For instance: 'Yes, I can tell you about funding arrangements for postgraduate courses. I would like to come back to that later, though, once we have clarified whether a postgraduate course is right for you at this time.'

The appropriate times to offer information are:

- in response to a request;
- as a form of challenging – for example: 'You say your family circumstances mean you need to stay at home, but most of the jobs in the field which interests you involve travelling round the country. Could we look at this apparent conflict a bit more?';
- to facilitate the action-planning stage.

There are also times when it is appropriate to limit the provision of information:

- when the adviser senses that the client uses a request for information in order to avoid facing her emotions;
- when the adviser is having difficulty with what is happening and is tempted to escape into information giving. All experienced advisers will recognise this temptation, which is particularly strong under pressure of time, or pressure of client panic.

We have placed the skill of providing information in the interpretative skills portion of the pyramid quite deliberately, because it offers the adviser such a high level of influence. What is selected and how the information is given will significantly influence how the interview proceeds. Although information could in fact be offered at any stage of the interview, its power and influence may be so great that it should, like the other interpretative skills, be used sparingly and at the later stages of the exchange, once the developmental issues have been explored and clarified.

The next chapter examines how these skills can be integrated with the model in specific situations with clients.

Chapter 6

Application of the model and skills in the careers interview

Chapter 4 described a particular model for the careers interview and Chapter 5 described specific counselling skills required for working with this model in a careers context. It is of course impossible to use these skills in isolation, to bring them out with a flourish when the adviser feels like it. They are part of the overall approach. The adviser will adopt counselling skills in her own personal interview model, and they will be in place at the beginning and throughout the interview. As we have seen, some of the skills are fundamental in establishing the essential empathy which is the basis for the introduction of the other skills. The level to which the skills at the top of the skills pyramid (see Figure 5.1) are used depends on the needs of the client at that moment. For certain careers interviews the skills of immediacy and self-disclosure may not be necessary or appropriate, but in full-length interviews the adviser will draw on appropriate skills as the interview deepens and progresses. There is no way of knowing at the beginning to what depth the adviser and client will need to go, and so for each interview the foundation of empathy must be laid by the effective introduction of listening and understanding skills throughout.

This chapter looks at a number of strategies drawn from practical experience which demonstrate the integration of counselling skills into the chosen interview model. It is of course not comprehensive; but some examples demonstrate where we have developed ways of moving the client forward. Experienced advisers will no doubt recognise some of their own strategies here. It is hoped that less experienced advisers will be able to draw on the examples to make sense of their developing professional practice.

You will remember that this model has four phases in a dynamic relation to one another, with each one having a number of specific tasks. We shall now consider some strategies and skills which enable tasks to be achieved during each stage: clarifying, exploring, evaluating and action planning.

STRATEGIES DURING THE CLARIFYING PHASE

The tasks in the clarifying phase are to set the scene, to develop empathy, to hear the story and to make an initial assessment.

Whatever the circumstances, it is essential that the adviser communicates the key values on which the exchange will be based. If the client senses that his feelings and beliefs will be heard and understood, then he will be enabled to play an active role. How the adviser begins will depend on the particular circumstances of the time available, the location of the interview and the initial assessment of the client's needs. In other words there is no set formula for starting the interview, as this would certainly appear artificial and contrived, but there is a certain similarity about the more 'basic' kind of beginning.

In this 'basic' open beginning, the client has made the first contact after arranging an appointment.

Adviser: We have about three-quarters of an hour to work together. This is your time to use as you want. Where would you like to begin?

The adviser indicates the time boundaries and the client is encouraged to use the time to concentrate on what is important to him.

In this more challenging beginning, the client has just been rude to the receptionist after learning he has been rejected by yet another employer.

Adviser: You sound very angry about all this. Perhaps you would like to start today by talking about how you are feeling.

The adviser acknowledges and demonstrates understanding of the strength of feelings.

In this example of a more focused beginning, aiming to open things up, the client has been referred by a guidance teacher to discuss nursing as a career opportunity.

Adviser: Your guidance teacher tells me you would like to find
out more about nursing. Perhaps you could tell me
where you would like to start?

The adviser acknowledges the referral and the specific nature of
the interview, but the client is gently given the opportunity to
confirm that this is what he wants to talk about and what aspects
are important. The adviser is starting where the client is at that
time, and will clarify how much the client already knows.

Clients arrive at interview at varying stages of career and
personal development. This will depend on their life stage, their
past experiences and their current circumstances. Reasons
expressed for arranging a careers interview vary accordingly. Just
a few include:

- 'I have no ideas.'
- 'My tutor said I should come.'
- 'I have a few ideas.'
- 'I know what I want to do – but how do I get there?'
- 'I need help with this application form/my CV.'
- 'All my flatmates have been.'
- 'I've got to find a job. The bank manager is hounding me.'
- 'I thought I had a place on this course but I've been turned
  down for funding.'
- 'I've failed my exams, what can I do now?'
- 'I don't like my course. I want to change.'
- 'I've just done this computer guidance thing and I don't know
  what to make of it.'
- 'I hate my job. I need to make a change.'
- 'My dad died last week. I need to get a job.'

The adviser must start with the issues first presented by the
client.

Analysis of this list of possible presenting issues identifies four
possible kinds of client an adviser could face at the beginning of
an interview:

- the vague client;
- the reluctant client;
- the client with a specific issue;
- the client in a crisis.

The vague client

Sometimes, no matter how open and gentle the introduction of the adviser, the client responds with a closed statement or question. This may arise from genuine confusion about the nature of a careers interview and what to expect from the careers adviser. The client may be taken aback by the open, cooperative approach, previous experience of such exchanges having led him to believe it will all be done for him (or to him) by the adviser. This may result in the client responding with vague statements such as:

- 'Well I've really not got any ideas.'
- 'Maybe you will tell me what I'm suited for.'

Right from the start it is useful to encourage the client, firmly if necessary, to open up and find a starting place without the adviser reinforcing the erroneous expectations by too obviously taking control. A variety of strategic responses may help the client become engaged in the process. In response to 'I have no idea of what I want to do', the adviser could reply:

- 'Maybe you can tell me what you don't want to do.'

or
- 'What sort of things have you already considered?'

A *short* description of the process of making career choices – looking at self and jobs, relating these to each other and developing transition skills – *can* serve to clarify the roles of adviser and client and encourage the involvement of the client. But there is a danger, however, that the strategy may reinforce the passivity of the client, particularly if the adviser lapses into narrative and does not check the client's understanding of the process described.

The reluctant client

This is the client who has been told by parents, teachers, tutors or social security officials that he must see the careers adviser. This is a difficult situation for the adviser who is trying to work with a client who will resist any cooperative moves and may not permit the development of empathy. If a client is not prepared to work on appropriate issues, all the skill in the world will not get him there. But if his feelings are recognised, then he can begin to let his fears and confusion show.

Nick:	My tutor told me to come.
Adviser:	You sound pretty angry about that.
Nick:	Yes, it's as if he's forcing me to make decisions.
Adviser:	Perhaps you're not ready to make decisions.
Nick:	Yes. I've got so much going on in my life just now it's difficult to cope with today, let alone think of tomorrow.
Adviser:	Mmm – tomorrow?
Nick:	Well, I don't like thinking about the future when I don't know what's going to happen ...
Adviser:	Mmm ... perhaps you can tell me about some of the things that frighten you about the future?

The adviser is gently building empathy by allowing the client to express his resentment and provides the opportunity for him to begin to tell his story.

The client with a specific issue

On the face of it, these clients seem to be the most straightforward. The issue appears to be clear and may simply involve the provision of information. For instance:

- 'I want to be a merchant banker.'
- 'I need help with my CV.'

As we have seen in Chapter 5, however, these specific issues are sometimes not as clear as they seem. The client may be testing the adviser – what sort of person is this? what can she do? Can I tell her more?

Alternatively, the client may believe a careers adviser expects to have a specific issue to work with. Rather than taking the issue at face value, the adviser will check out its reality with the client. Sometimes this can be done very easily:

Adviser:	What sort of jobs will you apply for with this CV?
Sue:	Well, I don't know yet. I thought I would just get it ready.

The issue may be more obscure with other clients:

Adviser:	Perhaps you could tell me what it is about merchant banking which appeals to you?
Dan:	Well, I know someone who started it last year. He seems to like it. There's lots of money and a lot of

contact with people. He was always very competitive, though. I'm not like that. Do you think it matters?

Here the adviser's open question encourages the client to begin to talk, to reflect on himself and begin to introduce some of his own self-doubt.

Of course, in most cases it is perfectly possible that the specific issue is exactly what the client needs to discuss. A skilled, sensitive adviser will be able to detect the different client needs.

The client in a crisis

Crisis points are not necessarily the best times for an adviser to be working with a client to promote the individual's self-growth and understanding. There is a desire to make decisions rapidly and often in an irrational way. A crisis, however, can enable a client to see things in new ways and to face up to issues which have been buried until now. There is often a great deal of emotion around – panic, anger, fear, shame. Once again, the acknowledgement of these feelings is an essential prerequisite to the developing empathy. To enable someone to voice the extent of his fear or anger can be the first step in developing the client's ability to cope with the feelings and to use the crisis as a transition point (see Chapter 3).

For example, this client has failed his exams and will now have to discontinue his course.

Adviser: It sounds as though you are feeling really scared about leaving college and facing the outside world. You see yourself as a student and it's frightening to imagine yourself in any other way.

During the clarifying phase, the adviser will draw on a number of skills to assess the client's level of vocational maturity (Chapter 4) and how much he has developed his self-knowledge, job knowledge, decision making and transition skills. Active listening will enable the client to provide some of the clues, while the skills of paraphrasing, summarising and questioning will confirm or correct the adviser's initial perceptions. The use of questions should be limited at this stage – too much direct probing could confuse the empathic sense of shared responsibility and could return the client to the passive role (see Chapter 5). The direction of the interview will be determined by the adviser's assessment of the client's stage and needs at this point.

This assessment is made during the first stage of the model and identifies the needs of the client in terms of self-knowledge, job knowledge, decision making and transition.

It is useful for the adviser to voice her perception of the client's position in order to initiate a relevant contract:

- To a client lacking appropriate self-awareness: 'It sounds as if you are not really clear yet about what is important to you in a job.'
- To a client lacking information about the nature of jobs: 'It sounds as though you have some ideas about what is important for you in work, but you haven't yet got a clear idea of what is involved in a range of jobs.'

STRATEGIES DURING THE EXPLORING PHASE

The tasks in the exploring phase are to build the contract, to explore the issues within the contract, to encourage the client to explore other issues, and to re-examine the contract.

As the interview progresses, there is a need for the adviser to negotiate a contract to encourage the client to be more specific about herself and her ideas and to move on to seek evidence to demonstrate what is important to her.

There are several strategies which an adviser might adopt at this point.

Explanation of the link between self-knowledge and the job search

This should preface the use of any of the other strategies, but may be enough on its own to engage the client in the task.

Adviser: In order to be able to relate yourself to possible job options, it is important to have a clear idea of what is important to you in a job. We could explore some of these factors now – what interests you, what you are good at, the way you like to think, how you interact with other people. What do you think about that?

It is vital that the adviser avoids the use of jargon at this point – unless the client obviously has an understanding of the words in a careers context. Terms like 'values', 'skills' and 'personality factors' all have connotations drawn from elsewhere which will influence the client's interpretations. If the adviser uses jargon, he must spell out what he means or run the risk of taking the expert role, taking more control and losing the client's cooperation.

Relevance of past experience

Here the client is encouraged to seek clues for herself from her past experience which will help to identify what is important for her.

Adviser: Let's look at the vacation jobs or work experience you have had, as the past can often give clues about the future. Perhaps you can identify what you were particularly good at (or particularly enjoyed, or what you learned from the experiences).

Introduction of guidance tools

The tools available to a careers adviser include pencil and paper exercises, computer-aided guidance systems and psychometric tests. Their relative advantages and disadvantages are explored in greater detail in Chapter 9.

Whatever the client's level of self-knowledge, the adviser will also have to explore how much she already knows about the world of work. The client who says she has no ideas or is not interested in anything may in fact have considered some areas but rejected them on the basis of false or insufficient knowledge. Individuals acquire information about different types of work in a myriad of ways from more or less realistic or biased sources:

● from family (e.g. where both parents follow the same profession the client will often have a very one-sided view of what the work entails);
● from teachers – whose motivation will vary;
● from friends doing different jobs;
● from working experience, e.g. observing others doing different jobs;

- from the popular press and television;
- from careers information sources – such as books, articles, computer databases.

Some of this information will be valid, and some of it will be biased and stereotyped and reinforce existing prejudices; e.g. 'Chartered accountancy is boring and involves nothing but numbers.'

The adviser's role is to help the client to explore the current concepts she has about different jobs in an effective way. This may be the stage where the adviser introduces a gentle challenge to help the client understand and perhaps challenge the source of her views and opinions.

Adviser: You tell me your mother has discouraged you from applying to the Civil Service.

Julia: Yes, she was a clerical officer before she was married. She says there are no career promotion prospects. It's just a dead-end job.

Adviser: I suppose that may have been so when she was working there. I wonder if it would be worth finding out if it has changed at all.

The best way of improving job knowledge when a client is beginning to focus on a specific area is to encourage her to make contact with people working in that field and to attempt to gain some experience – perhaps through voluntary work or short courses or work-shadowing. Many Careers Services have lists of local contacts.

Careers advisers whose clients are still in education can encourage them to make the best use of their time by gaining relevant experience through voluntary work, or help them arrange work-shadowing through their local contacts.

The need to acquire more effective decision-making skills may well emerge as the client's story unfolds and the level of self- and job knowledge becomes apparent. Some indication will be gained by understanding how the client has made decisions in the past – for instance, choice of course on leaving school, choice of first job. If this is the first major decision a client has to make as an adult, then this will be the area where she most needs the skills of the adviser. If there has been previous difficulty, it can feel quite over-powering if the current decision is not clear-cut. The adviser needs to acknowledge the strength of feelings around the decision making and offer support in the process. The resulting decision may involve a sense of loss of the option(s) rejected and the client may need to clarify and come to terms with her feelings about this.

Adviser: It sounds as if you are feeling quite scared about making these choices.

Chris: Yes. I've just realised I've never had to make such a big decision before. I'm afraid I'll get it wrong.

Adviser: Well, let's see if we can take it step by step and then we can look at what 'wrong' might actually mean.

While the adviser develops the process of the interview, the pace at which it progresses is dictated by the client. If she is not ready to get in touch with personal feelings about a particular issue, then no manner of skilled challenging will move her in this direction. Indeed the empathy may crumble and the client will raise barriers of resistance to take its place. An aggressive challenge will effect this instantly. It is probable that resistance is *always* present and can be used positively or negatively. Consider the relative effectiveness of the following two approaches.

Adviser A   So your results are pretty poor. Yet you still
[less   say you want to go to university. Their standards
effective]:   are high. How are you going to convince the course tutors to let you in?

Paul: I don't know.

Adviser B   So your results are poorer than you expected. How
[more   do you feel about it?
effective]:

Rachel: Well, I'm really disappointed. I had worked hard, but my gran died the week before my exams. I suppose that put me off a bit. I still would like to go to university – perhaps I should resit the exams.

The first adviser by the nature of her comments has implied that there is little to be done. The client closes up – he feels there is no point in discussing it. The second adviser acknowledges the feelings which the client must have at this point and with a very open question gives her the opportunity to reveal the information which might be helpful in exploring and beginning to resolve the issue.

STRATEGIES DURING THE EVALUATING PHASE

The tasks in the evaluating phase are to challenge inconsistencies, to enable the client to weigh up the pros and cons for each option, to prioritise options with the client, and to re-examine the contract. Sometimes the adviser's own sense of impatience may be indicating that she feels the pace is too slow. This is where a paraphrase or summary will effectively draw together the strands of what the client is saying and allow forward movement to occur. The adviser should manage her own impatience. The client is likely to interpret any communication of impatience as his fault and become confused in his attempts to move more quickly than he feels appropriate. Challenging is usually less effective if the adviser is already irritated.

Consider these two examples.

Adviser C [impatient]:	We'd better move on – we only have three-quarters of an hour and I've got someone else waiting at half past. What you are saying is very interesting but maybe we should look at some other options.
Ken:	Yes, maybe . . .

Adviser D [more patient]:	Let's see where we've got to. You've talked about what you enjoyed in your last job and why you left, and then we explored one or two ideas you had about the kind of work you would like to do now. Could we begin to look at how you might get into these areas?
Nora:	Yes, I'd like to look at . . .

The first adviser has a very real concern that the process of the interview will not be complete by the end of the allotted time. Unfortunately she conveys this concern with irritation to the client, who is likely to feel what he is saying is not very worthwhile. The second adviser also has concerns about the timing, but a brief summary of what has been said values what has gone before and gently moves the interview on.

During both the exploring phase and the evaluating phase, there is a number of common situations which the adviser may face. Clearly the progress of *every* interview is different but advisers will recognise some of the following difficult situations.

- the resistant client;
- the bitter client;
- the 'stuck' client;
- the unaware client.

The resistant client

There is really no other way of dealing with such a client apart from recognising where he is. This model and the associated counselling skills are person-centred and it is not possible to impose a method of working on a client. Resistance is always present to some extent, but when it is strong it may be derived from a variety of sources – real fear of change or of uncovering something difficult, considerable difficulty in expressing feelings, a personal dislike of the adviser (the so-called personality clash) or any other reason which is valid for the client. Previous examples have described how the adviser can work to encourage such a client to work at a deeper, more effective level, but there may come a point where it is clear that this cannot happen. The adviser should openly summarise and acknowledge the situation in order to move on. For example:

Adviser: I explained to you earlier how it could be appropriate to look at your feelings about your redundancy, but you've made it clear that you do not want to do this. I guess you will have your reasons, but it's my hunch that these feelings may get in the way of further exploration. This is of course your choice, so perhaps you could tell me what you would like to do with the time we have together now?

The adviser's tone of voice and body language must not be accusatory but must demonstrate acceptance that it is the client's choice.

The bitter client

The task of the adviser in this situation is first to recognise that the issue is real for the client, whether or not it may exist in fact. For example, a client may believe he is suffering from discrimination as a result of his race, disability, social background, age or any of a number of other factors. Discrimination exists, but some people tend to use this or even see it when it is not there, as a way of reinforcing a kind of trap of bitterness and repressed anger.

It can be very difficult to help such a client move on from the issue and he may constantly return to it unless the associated feelings are brought out into the open. For instance:

Adviser: You sound really angry at the idea that employers might reject you as soon as they see you are black.

Tony: Yes, it is so unfair. I'm just as well qualified as anyone else.

It is also essential for the adviser to help the client sort out how real the issue actually is. In some cases, there may be legal action which can be taken, although the burden of proof is on the client. Where there is no legislative protection, e.g. where discrimination is connected with age, the adviser's task is to help the client come to terms with the problem and to seek ways of working around it.

Adviser: You are right. It is difficult to convince employers in this field that a more mature candidate could have special value. Perhaps we could look at strategies for getting into the field through other, less direct, routes. For example, some mature people have started in smaller organisations where their flexibility is valued. Sometimes experience can be gained elsewhere which is relevant. Maybe a stepping stone approach could be effective for you.

Here the adviser recognises that there is a problem, but helps the client to move on by providing appropriate information and suggestions of a way forward, encouraging rather than getting bogged down in an 'Isn't it awful' approach.

It is sometimes the case that the client will use the issue to avoid taking action, implying that there is no point as it is out of his control. This behaviour is difficult for the adviser to work with. Whatever suggestions are made, the client uses a blocking tactic, such as 'What's the point? They wouldn't even consider me anyway.'

The adviser will stop this at an early stage to avoid reinforcing the pattern. One way is to use immediacy to focus on the feelings present.

Adviser:	Everytime we begin to explore the way forward, you seem to prevent yourself from considering any possibilities. I'm just wondering what is holding you back.
Fay:	I don't know.
Adviser:	Sometimes when we are afraid of what might happen in the future, we find a way to stand still. It seems to me that this might be happening here.

The adviser challenges the client's behaviour, giving him an opportunity to work out for himself what is going on. When the client is unable or unwilling to do this, the adviser puts forward one option in a tentative manner.

Simon:	But I said, as soon as they know I've been in prison they will not want to know.
Adviser:	We always seem to come back to this. You are sounding really angry as you say it.
Simon:	Yes. I am angry. OK, I did wrong, but I did my time – it was only the once. They will not let me put it behind me.
Adviser:	You feel you're still being punished.
Simon:	It's more than that. I'm marked for life for one stupid mistake. Why did I let myself get drawn into it?
Adviser:	That sounds as if you are angry at yourself as much as employers.

By focusing on the feelings present, the adviser enables the client to explore what might be holding him back from making decisions.

The 'stuck' client

This is a common problem. No matter how hard the adviser works, the client always seems to return to the same sticking point, managing to make the adviser feel useless. The counselling skills of challenging and immediacy can provide the basis of a strategy for moving the client on.

This client, for example, has worked hard on identifying important factors for him in his choice of job. He has completed an interest guide, but is unable to relate to any of the job suggestions. The adviser has tried to clarify other factors influencing his decision making but every suggestion produces a 'Well, maybe' response. When the adviser points this out, she notices the client's eyes fill with tears.

Adviser: You seem very distressed right at this moment.
Alan   Yes. I just feel so frustrated. It doesn't matter what I
[The   do, whether I work with the computer, or talk with you
tears   about it, I just keep going round in circles and never
fall]:   get anywhere.

At this point the adviser must be wary of feeling threatened or challenged or overwhelmed. It may seem that the client is accusing the adviser of not providing a solution. It is, however, his own inability to move on which is causing the distress. It is the adviser's responsibility to respond to the distress in an empathetic way in order to help the client make sense of it.

Adviser: It seems as if something is blocking you from making
          decisions.
Alan: Yes. I ought to be able to decide but I just can't make
          up my mind.
Adviser: Ought?
Alan: Yes. Well, all my friends are getting 'good jobs with
          prospects', and my parents, well, they just want me to
          be happy, but they mean a settled job with a career
          ladder.
Adviser: It sounds as if you have several drivers – your friends
          and your wish to be like them, your parents and your
          need to please them, and, inside, yourself. The drivers
          may be conflicting. I wonder if that is what is blocking
          you?
Alan: That may be right. I suppose I should concentrate on
          what I want now – I've always done what others
          thought was best for me.

The unaware client

Early in the interview it may become clear that making effective applications and performing well at interviews represent most difficulty for the client, especially where there is direct evidence of a problem; e.g. failure to gain any interviews or failure to perform well at interview. Strategies in these cases can be fairly straightforward. The client can be encouraged to reflect on past experiences of making applications and attending interviews to try to determine what has happened. The adviser should first check whether the client has already sought feedback from employers. Practice varies, but some employers are prepared to explain why an application has failed.

An explanation of the normal process of selection by employers can begin to help a client to see the process from a different angle and the client can be encouraged to put himself in the shoes of the selector.

Adviser: Employers will generally draw up a job description from their knowledge of the task required for the job. From that description they develop a person specification which details the desired skills and experiences, bearing in mind it is unlikely that they will find the 'perfect' candidate.

   Looking at your application, what similarities and differences are there compared to what the employers are looking for?

or

   Perhaps we could draw up such a person specification for this job together and then see how you could show how well you fit in?

This is an effective strategy where it is patently clear to the adviser that the client is either under-selling himself on paper or at interview, or making unrealistic applications in terms of his skills and experience. In the latter case, the adviser should be wary of communicating that the client will definitely not make it. Experience has shown that strange things can happen in the selection process. An employer can be so impressed by a client's motivation that a job is created for him.

Experiential learning can be one of the most effective strategies for helping the client to be more realistic. Where circumstances permit, the adviser can offer a mock selection interview. The mechanics of this are described in Chapter 9.

It is much more difficult, however, to raise a client's awareness of poor presentation skills, particularly potential difficulties in a selection interview, where the client is *unaware* of having specific problems. The early exchanges in the guidance interview may clearly demonstrate to the adviser that this client will have difficulty promoting himself. On one level the client may have difficulty in controlling the volume of what is said, may not listen, may interrupt frequently, or may not keep to the point. On another level there might be evidence of poor eye contact, poor articulation with a strong regional accent, even poor personal hygiene or inappropriate dress styles. The task of the adviser is to make the client aware of the potential difficulty in a safe, constructive manner. No assumption should be made that the client is completely unaware of the problem but even if he is, he may never voice it if the adviser does not provide the opportunity. This involves the skills of challenging and immediacy once essential empathy has been established.

This client does not keep to or address the question:

Adviser: Can I stop you there for a moment? I'd like to give you some feedback on what seems to be happening here because I think it might influence how employers will perceive you.

Several times in our discussion you have had some difficulty in sticking to the point. For example, we agreed you would tell me about your last job in the library, but you are now giving me your opinions on government pay policy. I'm wondering how an employer might react to this?

The adviser approaches the challenge very tentatively, but uses immediacy to provide a specific example which leaves the client in no doubt about what the adviser means.

Another client is applying for jobs in the retail industry, but clearly has a personal hygiene problem:

Adviser: I feel I should raise an important topic which we all find difficult to talk about. We've mentioned that this type of work involves meeting the public. Sometimes when we are under stress we have a problem with body odour and I notice today that you seem to have such a problem. I know it's difficult for you, but perhaps we could talk about it.

Again, the adviser approaches the issue tentatively, acknowledges its difficulty but is very specific. The challenge given is based on fact, but is not accusatory and moves towards supporting the client in dealing with a factor which will be very important in the personal interactions of the job search.

STRATEGIES DURING THE ACTION-PLANNING PHASE

The tasks in the action-planning phase are to help the client identify what needs to be done, to encourage the client to formulate an appropriate systematic plan of action, to introduce the concept of referral if necessary, and to end the interview.

It is probable that a good proportion of careers interviews do not result in the client selecting some career option(s) to explore. Career choice is a process. The interview is an intervention to enable that process. If a major issue emerges partway through the interview, it may be necessary to renegotiate the contract with the client and use the available time to work on that issue, which then becomes part of the overall developmental process.

The action-planning phase could then involve a referral to another practitioner to continue to work to a greater depth, before career decisions are made. Wherever possible, the needs of the client should determine the pace and focus of the interview. There is no point in trying to develop a long-term career strategy if the concern dominating the client's thoughts and feelings is about the break-up of his marriage.

Adviser: In our time today, we've begun to look at how you might change your career direction. In that process we recognised that you have a lot of confused feelings about your marriage breaking up and we agreed that you will begin to address these with a counsellor. I'm now wondering how much you want to continue to explore career options at this point.

Ben: It has become clear that my dissatisfaction with my job is possibly linked to the other things happening in my life, so maybe I should wait a bit on this one.

Adviser: OK. That seems sensible at this point. You can contact me when you feel ready to move on.

Where the adviser suspects that the client will want to prolong the interview, it can be appropriate at this point to draw attention to the time constraints in order to focus on the need for ending.

Adviser: We have ten minutes left of our time together. Perhaps we could use this to summarise where we have reached and what your next step will be?

The ending should be conducted firmly, but not abruptly. Where strong feelings have been expressed, the client needs time to draw back and to adjust to the idea of moving into the world outside the interview room again. The adviser should recognise this need and check this out with the client.

Adviser: How are you feeling now?
Anna: I'm still a bit shaky, I think.
Adviser: Perhaps it would be useful to plan what you are going to do for the next hour or so.
Anna: Yes, I think I'll go and sit in the library for a while. I'm not ready to go back to work yet.

SUMMARY

This chapter has explored a range of strategies (drawn from the authors' own practical experience) which will enable the adviser to integrate counselling skills into the guidance model. Clearly, every adviser–client relationship is unique and the skilled adviser will learn through experience how to develop and implement her own strategies in a natural and appropriate way for each individual client, whatever the context. Chapter 10 demonstrates how some of these strategies are actually used within one guidance interview.

Whatever the needs of the client and the skills of the adviser, no careers interview takes place in isolation. In the next chapters we shall consider the possible effects of the wider environment in which the interview takes place and the challenges which that environment can pose to the individual.

Chapter 7

The immediate environment

No client who seeks guidance comes as an isolated unit, capable of making the most logically 'correct' career decision in a vacuum. Everyone comes with a complex of personal circumstances which will have a bearing on how their career pattern will develop. Sometimes these personal circumstances act as powerful motivators to individuals to aspire to achieve large ambitions, but sometimes they act as pressures which the client feels as a burden or as a distortion from her preferred route through life. It is the careers adviser's role to get a sense of the wider picture against which the career decisions are being made. Sometimes all the significant issues may be so closely intertwined in the client's mind that any consideration of her career needs will inevitably touch upon a whole set of surrounding circumstances.

The skilled careers adviser can offer the client the opportunity to disentangle the various strands of issues which need to be resolved and indicate which can be dealt with in the context of a careers interview and which might be addressed elsewhere – whether by the client alone, with friends or through personal counselling. This chapter deals with some of the issues arising from a client's personal circumstances which may be encountered in careers interviews.

The case studies which follow demonstrate the powerful influence which family members, peers and partners may have on the self-concept and thought patterns of clients who seek careers guidance. This chapter also examines the effects on career choice of changing family patterns which have destabilised traditional forms of relationship. Other undermining factors such as homelessness and debt may also impinge on a client's freedom of action, as can be seen from the concluding examples in the chapter.

SIGNIFICANT OTHERS

The term 'significant others' refers to people whose interaction with an individual have an important impact on his emotions, behaviour and life decisions. The feedback received from these people matter greatly to him. It is they who create the 'conditions of worth' mentioned by Carl Rogers by setting parameters for how the individual perceives that he should act in order to be acceptable to them. Such is their influence that they can cause him to adapt his 'self-concept' if their view of him appears to be at odds with their own.

In a careers interview it is often important to explore to what extent the client's thinking on career issues is being shaped by the views of significant others. Where another person is, for instance, providing a role model which spurs a client on to succeed, this influence may be entirely beneficial. On the other hand, where the client is abdicating responsibility for decision making in deference to a dominant partner or parent, then it may be appropriate to challenge the decision. Similarly, where a client is proposing to follow a line of action contrary to his own wishes because of perceived, external pressure, then the adviser may wish to raise the client's awareness of his reasons for opting for a particular route.

The following examples indicate some of the pressures which significant others can bring to bear on individuals and demonstrate how a careers adviser can respond in order to make the client more aware of what is happening.

In all of these settings it would be highly insensitive of a careers adviser to state bluntly that other people's opinions do not matter and that the individual must openly assert his or her right to act independently. Freedom of choice is the ultimate aim of a careers interview. A counselling approach offers a way of exploring layers of constraint and feelings about relationships with other people which have hitherto prevented an individual from resolving problems and moving forward wisely.

Parents

Some of the tensest situations arise when maturing adults experience a serious mismatch between their parents' expectations of them and what they themselves want or feel capable of achieving. This can occur for a variety of reasons.

Some parents, when investing in their children's education, either through paying for private schooling or through supporting them through university, see themselves as 'making sacrifices'. When parents expect that their son or daughter will treat study and the subsequent job search as a serious matter from the start, then the young person may perceive a dilemma between satisfying parental demands and following his own personal route.

Case study: Nasrim

Nasrim's parents had worked extremely hard since settling in the UK to build up their small retail business. Their aspiration for their daughter, however, was that she should enter one of the professions. They had set their sights on her becoming an accountant – but Nasrim felt that she would be happier in a more creative job, using her hands.

Nasrim: I know that my parents work hard in the shop seven days a week and I should be grateful for the opportunity to get on in life – but I'm not sure I'm cut out for university. I would really prefer to be doing a practical job.

Adviser: It sounds as if I'm hearing echoes of what your parents say to you when they talk to you about going to university. But you don't sound convinced ...

Nasrim: Yes, my father harps on endlessly about how I'll be throwing all my chances away if I don't go to university. My mother doesn't say much, but I know she thinks the same. But they never really listen to what else I might want to do ... and I don't have the facts at my fingertips.

Adviser: I wonder how you could help them to understand that there are other viable alternatives?

Nasrim: Maybe I need to find out more about other options with good prospects apart from going to university.

Other parents may be tempted to try to live their own unfulfilled ambitions through their families. In such cases a child can be virtually brainwashed from an early age into accepting how wonderful it would be to become a doctor or an actor or a commando. Some young people may satisfy their parents' hopes in fulfilling their own ambition and the dream is then achieved for both generations. In other cases, however, a point is reached at which the young person has to acknowledge the fact that the lifestyle chosen for him by his parents is not working for him and to recognise his own lack of commitment at heart to this 'chosen' occupation.

Case study: Jeremy

Jeremy's mother worked as a secretary in a lawyer's office before she married and was aware of the social status of lawyers. His father was a shipping clerk who twice experienced redundancy as his employers' firms went bankrupt. Both of them were very proud of Jeremy's intelligence and hoped that the law would offer a passport to greater security for him than they had had in their working lives.

Aiming to become a lawyer was well within his grasp and his school was all too keen to encourage him towards this goal. By the end of his LL B. degree, however, Jeremy really felt at that point he would find a career in law very arid.

Jeremy: Well, I've done what they wanted. I've got a law degree – but the prospect of trailing around looking for a legal traineeship and committing myself to that way of life forever is just too awful for words. I get depressed just thinking about it.

Adviser: You seem to feel an obligation to do something which has no appeal for you. I'm wondering what makes you feel like that.

Jeremy: Yes . . . well, no, it isn't exactly an obligation, but I know that my parents always had a dream about me being a lawyer – to have a chance of the sort of lifestyle which they never had. I remember how pleased they were when I was accepted for law school. I would feel that I was letting them down if I didn't go through with it.

Adviser: 'Go through with it' sounds a bit grim – as if you would have to do it with gritted teeth and never really be free to enjoy your working life.

Jeremy: Yes, I suppose that is how I feel, really.

Adviser: I wonder if your parents realise how you are feeling?

Jeremy: I wouldn't talk about it. It would just cause upset – but it must be fairly obvious that I'm not enthusiastic about the next step.

Adviser: Sometimes things seem obvious to us because we feel them so keenly – but if we do not open up and talk plainly, it may be difficult for others to understand how it feels for us. Maybe we could explore how you could do that with your parents.

Sometimes parents can have difficulty accepting the fact that their children are not as intelligent/athletic/musical/business-oriented or otherwise talented as they would like or imagine them to be. This can result in parental expectations well beyond the young adult's capabilities, irrespective of any amounts of cajoling and extra tuition. Such a situation of low self-esteem can be exacerbated if parents, whether wittingly or unwittingly, hold up one sibling as an example to the others. The favoured child may either revel in or become embarrassed by this situation, which in itself can cause further tensions within the family.

Case study: Andrew

Andrew: I was really pleased for Jamie when he won a place at Sandhurst. He really deserved it and he's in his element there. But since then I'm fed up hearing about how wonderful it would be if I could follow in his footsteps.

Adviser: So, people are holding Jamie and Sandhurst up to you as a kind of role model.

Andrew: Well, not people generally – mainly my dad. He used to be in the Forces as a NCO and I think he regrets not having been able to go further.

Adviser: So, it's dad's idea that you should go to Sandhurst. How do you feel about that?

Andrew: It's an awful burden. I wish I could just do what I want.

Adviser: Well, let's explore that, then. You said you were fed up hearing about Sandhurst. I wonder if you have other ideas for your future?

Andrew: I'm not the action man type. My main interest is computing and I would like to do something in that line.

Adviser: That could be just as challenging in its own way as Jamie's cadetship at Sandhurst – and more suited to your talents. Maybe that is a point to bring into your next conversation with your father.

Partners

Similar feelings of pressure can exist in relationships between partners. If carried to extremes, the partners' mismatch of expectations can destroy the relationship. For instance, in some relationships one partner is much more concerned than the other about attaining a good standard of living, often coupled with aspirations to a certain social status. Sometimes the more ambitious partner has been dissatisfied with the occupational role of the other from the outset, but hoped to encourage a change in this. In other instances the standard of living drops dramatically and the social status is threatened when one of the partners loses a job and becomes unemployed. Because the status-conscious partner has viewed the other at least partly as a status symbol or provider of a standard of living and not solely for his or her own worth as a person, the relationship can be eroded without either party being fully conscious of what is happening.

Case study: Jane

Jane and Peter were a fairly traditional couple, with Peter clearly designated as the breadwinner. Jane's part-time job with a property firm was chosen so as not to interfere with her other responsibilities as mother and family social secretary. When Peter's business failed, both were faced with an unwelcome readjustment.

Jane: Peter inherited his father's business, but he didn't have his father's business acumen and when the recession began to bite, he didn't have the flexibility to diversify and make a go of it. So now we're bankrupt and I'll have to get a better job because he's floundering.

Adviser: It sounds as if you are feeling quite angry about the whole situation – and about Peter in particular.

Jane: Yes, I suppose I am angry. This isn't what we had planned. It has affected our whole lifestyle.

Adviser: And your lifestyle is very important to you ... to both of you?

Jane: I suppose I feel that more than Peter does. I suppose he's a bit shell-shocked at the moment ... but meanwhile, I suppose I could be doing something about it by getting a better job.

Some women feel, whether realistically or not, that success in a career is acceptable to their partner (and often to themselves) only if it can run alongside excellence in housekeeping, hospitality, motherhood and other roles, each of which can constitute a full-time occupation in itself. This can apply equally to a mature student, a business executive or a factory operative. In most cases this 'Superwoman syndrome' is associated with having perfectionist standards and is largely self-inflicted, but there are instances where the pressure from a partner is very real and the woman's response of doing several major jobs simultaneously may be seen as the price of keeping the peace at home.

Case study: Marie

Marie liked to have all aspects of her life under control – and to achieve excellence in everything. Most of the time she was successful. Friends marvelled at how she could build up a successful export business, chair a local businesswomen's group and still find time to entertain on a lavish scale. Following a particularly busy spell, however, her health had given way. Marie had to face the fact that being 'Superwoman' was no longer a sensible aspiration. She had tried very hard to achieve 'Superwoman status' in many areas of her life. However, the stress had finally got on top of her and she had 'crashed'.

Marie: I think this recent breakdown was due to the fact that I never had a minute to myself. Orders in the business were picking up and I had to be there to supervise overtime. But Harry's away a lot in his job and so a lot fell on my shoulders at home too – keeping the house ship-shape, chauffeuring the kids – the lot, really. I don't know if I can go back to that – and yet I would hate to give up the business now that it is proving successful.

Adviser: You have obviously invested a lot of time and energy in your business. It's part of your identity – and it is usually a good feeling to be associated with success. I wonder if there are ways in which you could keep the business and yet lighten the burden which you were carrying before your illness?

Marie: Well, I suppose I could delegate some of the overtime supervision – or maybe all of it if she wants the extra cash – to Sadie, my chief chargehand. She has been superb while I've been away. It would be a sort of promotion for her.

Adviser: And at home?

Marie: That's not so easy. Harry has been doing more lately, but I can't see that lasting.

Adviser: Maybe that needs to be discussed with Harry – along with other options, such as the children doing more – or bringing in outside help.

Marie: 'I don't like the idea of not supervising things personally, but maybe that's the price of keeping the business – and I really want to do that.

Adviser: It can be hard to let go of some of the control you've been used to having for yourself – but it can also give you new freedom.

In some situations one partner who has made more progress feels obliged, either out of sensitivity for the other or out of fear of the other's envy, to tone down his or her hard-won success. Some people turn down promotion because of fear it would upset the couple's lifestyle; for instance, by requiring longer working hours or a relocation. This is a situation that is still more commonly experienced by women than by men. It is virtually a dilemma between loyalty to self and loyalty to a partner. Whichever way it is resolved, it often means a sacrifice of one partner's career prospects. It may also highlight a difficulty in the relationship and bring it out into the open.

Case study: Connie

Frank and Connie had a basically good relationship, but Frank's loss of his job as a sales representative had badly dented his confidence. Although now in a part-time storekeeper job, he described himself as being 'between jobs', as a sign that he had higher aspirations.

Since Frank's redundancy, Connie's salary as an office supervisor had become a more significant proportion of the couple's income. When her company closed down the local branch, it looked as if the couple's bad luck was set to continue, but Connie's excellent performance had been noted and she was offered a promotion at the company's headquarters – over 200 miles away. Ostensibly, there was no real impediment, but feelings at home ran high.

Connie: I know I'm really lucky to have this opportunity. A lot of people are being made redundant when they close our office, but a transfer to head office will be a promotion for me . . . if only I were free to accept it.

Adviser: You say 'free'. Can you explain what you mean?

Connie: Well, it has caused such ill-feeling at home. I thought Frank would have been pleased as he is only working part-time and there would be better prospects for him elsewhere. But his whole attitude is putting a veto on the move. I wouldn't go without him – but it is galling to think that I'll be unemployed when I could have had a promotion.

Adviser: That doesn't *sound* a very good deal for you – or for Frank. Maybe it would be helpful for you to explore all the possible options – both here and in the new location before you speak to him about the future.

Connie then began to explore the possibilities and began to realise how apprehensive Frank was about change. She realised that she needed to do a bit more thinking about her own needs and ambitions and the realistic opportunities for them before talking to Frank again.

Peers

For most people the power of peer pressure is greatest in adolescence and early adulthood – for instance, peer pressure is a common occurrence at the secondary school stage. Sometimes it is seen as a 'weakness' to devote time to study – or even in extreme cases to attend school regularly. A bright teenager who, as parents would say, 'gets in with the wrong crowd', may pass up the opportunity to gain good qualifications and entry to a promising career for the sake of remaining acceptable to the social set, which at that time means more to him or her than academic success does. Such a person may subsequently regret that decision once other values in life have become important. This was the case for Martin.

Case study: Martin

Martin's school reports had always indicated that he had more intelligence than he cared to display. As a teenager it seemed more important to him to be street-wise than to gain qualifications which no one in his family or peer group particularly prized.

Occupations after school included working at open-air markets and selling secondhand cars at auctions. His most recent job had been selling car spares and accessories, but he did not see himself doing this for the rest of his life. At the age of 25 he was becoming more aware of lost opportunities.

Martin: I have nobody to blame but myself. You know what it is like when you are a teenager – you know best what is right for you. I could have had qualifications if I had gone to school even one day in three – but it was more attractive to hang out with the gang that played pool, or just roamed the streets.

Adviser: You obviously regret that time of lost opportunity, but it sounds as if you have written off your prospects for all time – which would be a pity.

Martin: I have at last got a bit of responsibility in the job which I have now, but I can't go much further without qualifications – and yet I can't afford to leave the job.

Adviser: You seem to have a very different attitude now to study.

Martin: That's right. Before there was no motivation to study. It just wasn't important to me ... but now I see qualifications as a way out of a dead end. A part-time course while working would be ideal.

Some students find it difficult to follow their own convictions and continue to be greatly influenced by what other people think and say. Students approaching the end of their courses frequently refer to pressure which they feel from their peers to apply for graduate training schemes and other 'mainstream, graduate-level' occupations. As a result, students who have not decided on what they want to do with their lives can find themselves applying to employers in the 'milkround' (campus recruitment visits) – often unsuccessfully, as their lack of commitment is frequently all too obvious to selectors. This lack of success further undermines their confidence in their own convictions and leaves them doubting their ability to succeed in any sphere.

Case study: Jim

Jim had enjoyed his languages degree, though his year abroad in a French school had shown him that he didn't want to join the teaching profession. For want of any other strategy he had begun to apply in his final year for jobs in finance and sales – mainly because employers advertised for graduates of 'any discipline'. He knew that his heart was not in any of the jobs for which he was applying – but he would have to do *something* after graduation to pay off his student loan. Maybe it was too much to expect to *enjoy* a job.

Jim: It's really demoralising to keep getting rejections. I'll never get a job if I cannot even make it to the interview stage.

Adviser: That's tough – and it does get you down. Maybe you have some idea of what's going wrong.

Jim: Some of the questions are awful. And even the so-called 'easy' ones leave me stuck for words.

Adviser: Can you give an example?

Jim: Well: 'Why would you be suitable for this job?'

Adviser: That's quite an obvious question that an employer would want to ask. Maybe you can explain what you find difficult about it.

Jim: Half the time I don't know if I would be suitable. I'm only applying because they will take graduates of any discipline.

Adviser: I don't understand why you would apply for jobs which don't interest you. Can you explain?

Jim: Panic, I suppose. You can't afford to be choosy.

Adviser: Maybe it would be better to invest the same amount of time in exploring which kind of job would suit you. You may even find that it is inappropriate for you to apply through the milkround. Would you like to explore that before we return to your applications?

In the course of his explorations Jim began to realise that 'peer pressure' had influenced many of the decisions he had made about his life. He became aware that it was time for him to begin to take more responsibility for his own decisions and actions.

CHANGING FAMILY PATTERNS

Since the 1960s there has been a change from the pattern of the nuclear family unit of two parents and their children living together, usually with the extended family of grandparents, aunts and uncles living in the same community. Many young people now leave the family circle at an early age to live independently. In the 1990s the proportion of single-person and single-parent households in the community has reached an all-time high, while divorce or separation affects one family in three. Meanwhile the number of elderly people living alone or in care rather than with their families has risen.

While there are many positive aspects of independent living, it can also mean that people are left to cope alone with situations in which at one time they might have expected to receive family support. Lacking this, they may have to turn to professionals in the 'caring services' for advice. As a result, careers advisers may hear from clients about some of the following situations.

Returning home

When a new graduate or other unemployed person has to return home primarily for financial reasons after having left the family circle and established an independent life-style, the readjustment to living together again can be extremely difficult for all concerned. This is particularly true if the individual's job search is protracted and the problems of living in close proximity are compounded by the job-seeker having little money and few remaining social contacts in the area. It was like this for Patrick.

Case study: Patrick

Following graduation, Patrick was obliged to give up his city flat and return to live with his elderly parents in his home village. Once the seasonal tourist jobs dried up at the end of the summer, he was at a loose end and seemed to be making no progress with his long-term job search. His parents' well-intentioned suggestions and anxious enquiries soon became yet another irritant in an unsatisfactory situation. With his frustration running high, Patrick felt trapped by his circumstances.

Patrick: Anyone would think I didn't want a job. It's a Catch-22 situation. There are no jobs where we live and I can't afford to move out and live in the city where I might have better prospects.

Adviser: So there's friction at home but you feel trapped there by financial problems. I wonder which of the two would be the easier problem to solve?

Patrick: I got on fine with my parents when I wasn't living with them. My lifestyle's different from theirs. They are so set in their ways.

Adviser: So maybe moving out again would be best all round to avoid souring the relationship. That brings us back to the financial problem. Any ideas about even an interim move to help you with that?

Patrick: I suppose it comes down to lowering my sights and taking some kind of stop-gap job. My fear is that I'll then get trapped at that level and never get anything better.

Adviser: I agree that this could be a danger – but less so if you have a plan for what you want to do long term and keep moving towards that end. On the whole, employers prefer to see that people have been working. Apart from that, it will restore your sense of independence – which seems to be one of the main concerns for you at the moment.

Family resistance

Another problem which stems ultimately from lack of family support and understanding is resistance from other family members to an individual's growth and change. This can take the form of decrying a person's cherished ambitions, openly doubting a mature student's capability of completing a course, stressing the competitiveness of the labour market or belittling the person's prospects of ever gaining advancement in a career. Such behaviour usually signifies a deeper-seated problem in the family relationship, but the immediate effect in terms of a person's career is to destroy self-confidence by a continuous stream of negative suggestions which may be difficult to overcome unless there is a trusted external source of positive reinforcement.

Case study: Josie

Josie's family could not get used to the fact that she was about to become a graduate and a grandmother in the same year. When Josie began her Open University studies, it had been for 'self-development' and the family had been quite indulgent about that, but her decision to work towards a career after graduating did not fit other family members' plans.

Josie: I'm just making tentative enquiries. I never thought about getting a job after my Open University degree, but now that the course is nearly finished I would like to have something useful to do. Just something part-time so that it doesn't conflict with domestic commitments.

Adviser: Maybe you could explain the extent of those commitments so that I can understand what is possible in terms of work.

Josie: My family are all grown up now, but they like to be able to call on me in emergencies – especially once the new grandchild arrives. My husband is not too keen on me taking on too much. He thinks the Open University has taken up a ridiculous amount of time. He reckons I don't need to work. I know my age is against me, but I would like to prove to them all that the studying has been worthwhile.

Adviser: It sounds as if it is other people who need the proof. I wonder how you feel about the value of your degree yourself?

Josie: Oh, I have no doubt. It has opened up my mind and shown me what I can do. That's really the other reason why I want a job. I know I could do it . . . but I suppose I still let others get in the way.

Help for the carers

A major problem facing people who cannot depend on the network of the extended family is that the care of children or elderly or sick relatives may prevent the carer from working even on a part-time basis. In the past, grandmothers who did not work outside the home were the answer to many to these problems, but today many of them may themselves be in paid employment or may live too far away to be able to help. Although this problem is most acute for people with very small children, it is often forgotten that children's attendance at school does not solve all the problems, as after-school care and the long school holidays can also be difficult to accommodate.

Case study: Sam

Sam was the sole carer of his three children following his wife's death. During the previous three years he had had to cope with many blows apart from his bereavement, including ill health in the family and the difficult decision to give up his job, which was a key part of his identity. More recently, he had felt the need to take steps to establish himself in work before his age began to tell against him. He also felt that life might be passing him by.

Sam: After my wife died, I tried to keep on my job, but my middle son had a lot of illness that year and it was tough on all of us. I was taking a lot of time off work and my employer's sympathy eventually ran out. After that I was on unemployment benefit, which meant a big drop in our standard of living. That was bad enough, but the psychological blow of the loss of my job after the loss of my wife seemed like the last straw. I felt I had lost my identity.

Adviser: That was a difficult decision to have to make – but you felt it was the right one?

Sam: Yes, I would do it again if I had to. The kids are top priority. It was the right thing at the time. But now I need to move on and I don't know where to start.

Adviser: Maybe we could begin by identifying what were your main problems before you gave up work and explore how these could be resolved.

Sam: My main problem before was lack of emergency child care. Now that I feel the children are slightly less vulnerable than they were just after their mother's death, I could look at various options that would leave me free to return to work.

HOMELESSNESS

Homelessness is a growing problem and one which affects people of all ages. Sixteen- and seventeen-year-olds are not entitled to unemployment benefit, nor can their parents claim family allowance unless they are continuing their studies. Many young people in these circumstances leave home, voluntarily or otherwise, and subsist as best they can with no fixed income or on a very small allowance which may be inadequate for rent, food and other necessities.

Unless they can find some way of getting accommodation, young people in this situation may be caught in a cycle of deprivation where they drop out of the labour market altogether and concentrate on living by their wits or on charitable donations. Many of these young people fall through the safety net of the statutory services, and careers advisers are increasingly encountering clients for whom homelessness is a very real issue.

Case study: Monica

Monica's parents split up when she was 14 years old. She and her brother went to live with their father, but Monica's relationship with him grew increasingly stormy and by mutual consent she left home at the age of 17. For a while she had a live-in job in an hotel, but she regarded that as slave labour and left before she had another job lined up. She was camping out in a friend's bedsit until she could find a place in a hostel.

A trail round employment agencies had not been very productive as she could offer no referees, but at last she had been offered an interview for a post of auxiliary in an old people's home.

Adviser: I get the feeling that your mind is not really on your interview, even though it is happening tomorrow.

Monica: I'm sorry ... I suppose I just don't feel there is much chance of getting a job. For a start, I have nothing suitable to wear.

Adviser: Maybe that can be overcome – but you sound defeated before you start. I wonder why?

Monica: I don't have much faith in employers. They're all the same. As soon as they see 'no fixed address', it's a turnoff. They reckon you're work-shy. It's so unfair.

Adviser: So you reckon that it's safer to shield yourself from disappointment by either not attending the interview or not allowing yourself to hope for a successful outcome?

Monica: No, I ... Well, I suppose that *is* what I'm doing ... but it's terrible to keep being turned down for something that is not your fault.

Adviser: I can understand that feeling. ... If I can understand that feeling, do you suppose that maybe *some* employers could understand it too? Maybe someone will relate to your ambition to build a new life for yourself. After all, you have more at stake than someone who has plenty of home comforts. That could be a powerful motivator.

Monica: Well, certainly I wouldn't give up a half-decent job. I would see it as my escape route. If I could just convince somebody to accept me ...

Adviser: That takes us back to how convincing you can be at the interview. Shall we look at that now?

A relatively recent addition to the ranks of the temporarily homeless are people whose homes have been repossessed following mortgage non-payment due to either unemployment or crippling bridging loans when trying to move from one property without being able to sell another. People in this situation are usually shocked to find themselves homeless, even if they are able quite speedily to arrange temporary alternative accommodation with relatives or a stop-gap place in a council's emergency accommodation.

Such a trauma can have long-lasting effects for the former house-holder, inflicting a severe blow to self-confidence in all aspects of life, including career prospects or job performance if the person is still in employment. In this situation, the issue of homelessness is never far from the person's thoughts and so is likely to surface in discussions about other aspects of life, including careers.

Case study: Bob

Bob had always been a good provider for his family. His job as a skilled mechanic had been well paid and he had recently moved into a bigger house in a residential area. Keeping up the mortgage payments had been no problem as long as there was overtime working, but that dwindled and the next stage was short-time working. Finally, there was a pay-off of workers in Bob's age group and his secure world seemed to tumble around his ears. The humiliation of having the house repossessed was a real blow to his pride.

Bob: That really knocked the stuffing out of me. To lose my job and my home all in the same year. It was as if the bottom had fallen out of my world.

Adviser: Yes, I can see that that was a real low point for you and your family.

Bob: It has seriously affected my confidence – and I'm sure that this shows through when I go for interviews.

Adviser: I can understand how your confidence took a battering, but if you can see it, the reality is that you *are* getting interviews. That's a hopeful sign. Perhaps the shock of redundancy has meant that you have lost sight of all the positive factors which you have to present to an employer. Maybe you could tell me what those factors are.

Bob: Well . . . I have a first-class track record in my trade – and experience of training others as well as doing the job myself . . .

DEBT

Just as careers advisers cannot directly assist homeless people to find accommodation, neither can they be expected to be debt counsellors. Indebtedness is so prevalent in society today, however, that they should be aware of the ways in which this problem may impinge upon clients' work, training plans or career prospects.

Being in debt is a powerful motivator for taking the first job that comes along, whether or not it is suitable in terms of the individual's interests and abilities. This is often the case with new graduates. A lower-level job offers at least some income and may therefore seem preferable to holding out for a more appropriate occupation.

Case study: Morna

Following her first degree, Morna had taken out a large loan for a postgraduate marketing course. On graduation she did not immediately find work and could not afford to accumulate any more debts. After placing a 'situation wanted' advert in a newspaper, she was contacted by an insurance sales firm. It was not the kind of job she wanted, but she felt obliged to take it as a temporary measure.

Adviser: So you don't feel you are cut out for insurance sales on a commission-only basis. Has your view changed since you took the job?

Morna: I wasn't very hopeful of it from the outset, but it was the first job that came along and the bank manager was hounding me to reduce my overdraft. I couldn't afford to go any deeper into debt.

Adviser: So it seemed a sensible move at the time – but it hasn't worked out for you.

Morna: I suppose I should have known that it wouldn't suit my personality. I hate having to persuade people into something they don't want. I'll never be any good at it.

Adviser: At least you are now clearer about what you do *not* want in your long-term career. Maybe we could analyse your reaction to this job to identify what you would prefer and then concentrate on how you might be able to move in that direction.

Another variation on this theme is the 'gilded cage' syndrome, experienced by people who acquire jobs with high salaries – for instance, in finance or with international organisations – and develop a lifestyle in which they are spending up to the limits of their salary – or beyond. If they subsequently become unhappy with their employment and wish to change direction, they may find that they are unable to find alternative work paying the kind of salary which is necessary to meet their commitments. Unless they are willing to alter their life-style radically, they remain trapped in a job which is no longer congenial.

Case study: Frances

At the age of 35, Frances seemed to have reached the top of the secretarial ladder in terms of salary and prestigious office accommodation. Her boss, however, was a former managing director who had clearly been shunted sideways by the younger generation in the firm. He seemed happy to maintain the appearance of being busy while coasting home to retirement, but Frances felt that there was no real substance to her job and that she could be an endangered species once her boss finally retired.

Frances: I would never get a secretarial job at this rate of pay anywhere else – and now that I have bought a flat and a nice car, I cannot afford to take a cut in salary. But I know I'll never be promoted here. They are so inflexible about career development for secretaries.

Adviser: It sounds like a case of conflicting priorities: a good salary, but no prospects; or take the risk of leaving in order to achieve more job satisfaction. I wonder if the salary or the job satisfaction has the higher priority at the moment?

Frances: I suppose the need for more job satisfaction has the edge – or I wouldn't be here today.

Adviser: That's what I detected from your earlier conversation. Maybe we can review some of the options open to you – some of which might result in higher earnings in the long term after an initial drop in salary.

A state of perpetual indebtedness can result in a person constantly moving on from one address and one job to another in an attempt to keep one jump ahead of creditors. Once this pattern is established and a CV reflects a series of short-lived appointments, employers become suspicious of the employee's reliability and it becomes more and more difficult for the person to remain in regular employment – which in turn accentuates the debt problem.

Case study: Carla

Carla and Mark seemed to have everything going for them. Stylish and confident, they were an attractive couple in the social scene and their whole lifestyle – with a sports car, an expensive flat and frequent holidays – seemed designed to impress. They both worked hard for these privileges, so why shouldn't they enjoy them?

The story changed, however, when Mark abruptly left home and a whole trail of debts came to light. Carla was left to pay the piper. She is now taking a postgraduate information technology course in order to increase her earning potential.

Carla: We were both irresponsible. Newly married and had to have everything at once – couldn't wait. I knew we were getting in over our heads, but I didn't know about the gambling debts until my husband left me to face the debt collectors.

Adviser: I wonder how you felt about that?

Carla: Panic-stricken – and angry. He had gone and I was left to pick up the pieces. I didn't know where to begin.

Adviser: It was then that you started to move from job to job?

Carla: Yes. There were orders for arrestment of wages and mortgage payments that couldn't be met. It was safer to keep moving on – but then employers became suspicious about all the short-term jobs, so I started to miss some of them out of my CV.

Adviser: I wonder what that was doing to your view of yourself as a worker?

Carla: I hated it. All the short-term jobs seemed to tar me with the brush of being shiftless and incompetent – which I'm not. I'm really good at my job, but I could never really launch into any of these recent jobs wholeheartedly because I couldn't feel secure about setting down roots.

Adviser: Now that a debt counsellor is helping you to sort out your finances, maybe you have ideas about how to win back some of your confidence and find a steady job?

Carla: I hope that completing the course which I am now taking will show that I can see something through to the end – and it will give me a current reference. That would be important in helping me to break the pattern of recent years.

SUMMARY

These examples give a flavour of the sorts of challenges from their environment which exist for clients when they arrive at a careers interview. They demonstrate that a career decision can rarely be taken in isolation from other important factors which make up the fabric of a person's life. If an attempt is made to do so, then the solution which does not take account of these key factors is likely to unravel like a badly sewn garment.

Many clients have no initial intention of discussing any issue other than their current job search or desire to change the direction of their career. Their expectation may be that the careers adviser will simply relay facts in relation to the availability of various types of jobs in the labour market. Once it becomes apparent that the adviser is trying to help the interviewee see the wider picture and to obtain not just any job, but a suitable match in terms of her skills, interests and temperament, then the client has a choice to make about how much to disclose of other life circumstances. It may then become clear that it would be pointless to consider jobs which would involve retraining or moving away from home, because of lack of finance or domestic commitments. The client may then choose to share more personal information with the adviser as she begins to recognise the relevance of such information to occupational choice.

Sensitive investigation of the broader picture can be of great service to a client by helping her to look at all the individual strands of a complex situation and to understand, perhaps for the first time, how they are inter-related. Once this is understood, it is possible for the adviser and the client either to move on towards a career plan against this backcloth, or to decide to defer an occupational choice or a change of job until other problems have been resolved. This resolution may be achieved through the client's independent actions or following consultation with other counsellors or agencies.

In this chapter we have considered the various individual circumstances which can come together to affect a person's career plan. In the next chapter we shall consider how the 'wider circumstances' of the labour market at any given time can affect an individual's position.

Chapter 8

The impact of the labour market

Developed economies are currently going through a transition which will change the nature of the employment market just as much as the Industrial Revolution did in its day. The concept of 'a job for life' is disappearing and the structure of the workforce is changing. People who are caught up in these changes often feel confused. If they find themselves unable to survive in a volatile labour market, they may begin either to doubt their own worth or to look for a scapegoat to which they can transfer responsibility for their lack of success.

The adviser's task is to try to help clients to make sense of their situation and to accept greater responsibility for their future whatever the circumstances. Careers advisers know about a range of economic and social factors which have a bearing on those circumstances. Ignoring these would not only defeat the purpose of guidance, which is to help a client to find a course of action appropriate to his situation, but would also prevent empathic understanding. This chapter examines some contemporary economic and social factors which are relevant to realistic guidance.

RESTRUCTURING OF THE WORKFORCE

Since the end of the 1980s organisations in both the private and the public sectors have been aiming to become 'leaner' and more cost-effective. This has involved them in a process which was initially termed 'down-sizing', but has recently been described more euphemistically as 'right-sizing'. The management theory behind this process is that it is possible for organisations to 're-engineer' their workforce in order to operate more efficiently and profitably while at the same time reducing the number of employees.

Many organisations which have 're-engineered' their structure have done so by cutting out tiers in the management hierarchy. The purpose of this redesign is to create more efficient organisations by avoiding the delays and potential for breakdowns in communication along an extended chain of command. Advocates of flatter structures aim to 'empower' teams of workers to take responsibility for their own productivity and standards of service delivery. They are also encouraged through 'quality circles' to become pro-active in analysing and resolving problems in the workplace in various innovative ways through team effort.

In some instances these developments have had all the desired outcomes and many staff feel a greater sense of ownership in the future of their organisation. Where these innovations have been less successful, however, they may evoke cynicism and workers may simply perceive that they have been given greater responsibility and bigger workloads while promotion prospects have been reduced.

Case study: Gordon

Gordon: Twenty years I've worked for that company. By now I should have had a reasonable expectation of a middle management job. And what do they do? Cut out middle management grades! Where do I go from here? At 45 they'll never see me now as a 'high flyer' – and so I'm basically stuck. But I have twenty years before retirement – unless they give me the chop as they've done with so many others. Where would I find another job at my age? What an outlook!

Adviser: So – you're feeling that all the efforts you have put in for the company over the years are counting for nothing. I expect you feel rather let down by that.

Gordon: Well ... I do in a sense. Oh, I know nobody owes me anything, but at least before I had hopes of some promotion. Now that is all swept away because these grades aren't there any longer.

Adviser: I wonder if you have been given a reason for the changes?

Gordon: It's supposed to be about improving communications and increasing productivity. They say it's about giving front-line workers more say in how things are run –

but if you ask me, it's about squeezing more work out of us for the same pay.

Adviser: So, you're feeling that you have lost your promotion prospects, but without gaining any real compensation. That certainly doesn't seem a good deal. I wonder how other people feel who have been affected by the regrading?

Gordon: It's not just me. Most people feel browned off about the changes ... but there's nothing we can do about it. It's out of our hands.

Adviser: That seems just the opposite of what the company says it wants to achieve ... yet you are being quite pro-active today in seeking to take control of your own future.

Gordon: Well ... maybe I've been too complacent in the past ... waiting for the company to give me promotion. Maybe I can do something to make it happen – or else move elsewhere.

PART-TIME WORK

In recent years there has been a marked rise in the proportion of part-time staff in the labour market. This has been particularly the case in occupations and sectors where women are in the majority – for example, in the retail, hotel and catering industries, among manual workers in the health service and in clerical posts in banks and building societies. Part-time contracts are also common for further education lecturers and tutorial assistants in universities.

Many women returning to the labour market after a career break take such part-time employment because it fits into their domestic circumstances, even though it may represent re-entry to the labour market at a level below their capabilities.

Case study: Margaret

Although she had been a highly efficient office supervisor in a pension fund management firm, Margaret's confidence about holding down a responsible job had ebbed away during the eight years when she was at home with her family. She knew that information technology had changed procedures in the financial sector and felt that her knowledge was out of date.

When she returned to work on a part-time basis, she therefore avoided posts which would expose her limited knowledge of computers and settled for a reception post which paid far less than she could have been earning had she remained in her previous employment.

Margaret: I knew that this job had no prospects when I took it. To that extent I can't say that they deluded me. The hours suited for the family coming home from school and it's a pleasant enough job being on reception. But what I didn't realise was that no one would take me seriously when I wanted to move on and get some training and promotion. I don't have access to any of that. I feel like a third-class citizen. I've really shot myself in the foot by taking that job.

Adviser: It sounds as if you feel that you have much more potential than you are given credit for. Perhaps you can tell me about that.

Margaret: I've always had a flair for working with figures – but there's no scope for that in my present job. At the same time I also get on well with people – whether it's customers or staff. In my last job I took a genuine interest in all the staff whom I supervised. Anyone who trained with me really knew the job inside out.

Adviser: You obviously have a lot to offer. I wonder if your present company realises how much it is losing out by not putting all this talent to use?

Margaret: Well, they probably don't know because they have never seen me working at full stretch.

Adviser: So they may not know that you have the potential to take advantage of further training, which would quickly repay the company's investment in you.

Margaret: I suppose that's true. Maybe I need to spell out more clearly what is the benefit to the company in offering me training – and be a bit more confident about my own abilities.

SHORT-TERM CONTRACTS

As with part-time staff, there has also been an increase in the proportion of staff who are on short-term contracts. This stems partly from employers' attempts to trim labour costs, but even where this is not the primary motive, employers may be reluctant to commit themselves to permanent contracts because of fluctuating business trends in the private sector and the short-term funding given by the government to local authorities and the voluntary sector. As a result, short-term contracts have become an increasingly common practice in the health service, local government, higher and further education, supply teaching in schools and voluntary organisations. They are also found among some multinationals (particularly for new graduate recruits), which want the flexibility of employing staff for the duration of specific projects or peaks of business activity. Some organisations have set themselves targets for reducing the core of permanent staff, who will in future be supplemented as required by a fluctuating population of temporary staff.

While temporary contracts can provide a good entry point into the labour market, a career founded on such terms tends to be insecure and has long-term implications for pension entitlement. The next case study shows the impact of short-term contracts on a highly qualified but insecure worker.

Case study: Heather

Heather had had a straight run through school and university to a first-class honours degree in politics and sociology, which she followed with a Ph.D. She had eagerly accepted a post-doctoral research post with her supervisor and that contract had eventually been extended for two periods of six months. As the second extension drew to a close, Heather was faced with compiling a research proposal to put before social science funding bodies with shrinking budgets – or looking around for alternative employment outside the academic sector. In respect of the latter she did not know where to begin.

Heather: Here I am – 28, qualifications as long as my arm – and I've never had a permanent job. When I graduated with my Ph.D., I was really flattered to be offered a post-doctoral fellowship, but it hasn't done me much good. I'm coming to the end of my third short-term academic contract and there's still nothing permanent in view. In fact, if our bid to the research council is turned down, I won't even have another short-term contract. It will be the dole queue.

It's not just the insecurity that bothers me – or the relatively low pay. I can't even get a mortgage because I don't have a regular long-term income. Academic work is what I want to do, but I might have to pack it in and take a job as some kind of management trainee – if anyone will have me at my age.

Adviser: It must be frustrating to have found the kind of work which you want to do and yet to feel prevented from doing it because of the surrounding circumstances.

Heather: Frustrating and also deeply annoying. I feel that I was encouraged down this path by the whole university culture – but it cannot deliver the goods in terms of a permanent research job.

But I have to face facts and try to look for alternative options. There must be *some*.

Adviser: Shall we look at those now? It sounds to me as if you have at least two main options. One is to remain in academic work in the hope of getting a permanent post eventually. You know that you enjoy the work, but the price-tag of that option is short-term insecurity.

On the other hand, you could explore what is open to you outside the university. You sounded fairly vague when you spoke about 'some kind of management trainee'. That makes me wonder to what extent you have explored all the other options.

Heather: Hardly at all. I knew I wanted to do postgraduate study and so I didn't waste time applying for jobs when I was an undergraduate. Then there was the post-doctoral post and I was happy with that. I'm not even too sure what I could do – or would want to do – outside of social science research.

Adviser: So you're not really aware of the options open to you and don't have enough information to judge whether you would find them satisfying. Could that be part of the reason why you feel so trapped at the moment?

Heather: I suppose so . . . I talk about other options, but I don't really have a clue about any of them – and so how can I relate to them?

Adviser: Maybe we can make a start by looking at some of the factors which would give you satisfaction in a job before moving on to consider which options would fulfil those needs. How does that sound as a starting point?

UNEMPLOYMENT

Unemployment is no respecter of gender, age, race or social class, but statistics show that some groups are more likely than others to be unemployed. These include residents in areas of urban deprivation, single parents, older workers, people with disabilities and health problems, members of ethnic minorities and, in the short term, new graduates with little work experience.

Apart from the economic consequences of unemployment, there can be serious psychological repercussions stemming from a sense of lack of worth and social isolation. Repeated rejections of job applications and failure at interviews may heighten the applicant's feelings of personal inadequacy and hopelessness. It is common for people who are long-term unemployed to feel victimised in a situation which is beyond their control. Ultimately, they may adopt a defence mechanism of not applying for jobs in order to avoid the pain of rejection. Alternatively, they may approach interviews carrying defensive feelings about their unemployment which may make it difficult for them to feel constructive about employment.

Case study: Stephen

After becoming unemployed at the age of 48, Stephen had completed a retraining course in the preparation of printed circuit boards. Quite a few of his co-trainees found work locally as a result of this course, but it was noticeable that the older trainees remained unemployed. Stephen drew his own conclusions from that and reckoned that his working days were effectively over, apart from occasional casual employment at polling stations and the like.

Stephen: I have to say that I haven't applied for much recently. There's not much point really. Employers want younger folk whom they can mould to their ways and who are prepared to go anywhere. It's just a waste of time filling out forms.

Adviser: I can understand your feelings about not getting anywhere. And yet there's no prospect at all if you don't apply. It sounds as if your enthusiasm is at a low ebb right now – and I can understand that too. No one likes to be rejected. I'm wondering what would help to restore your enthusiasm?

Stephen: Well, it would help if I could even get to the interview stage. I haven't had an interview for four months. It's like hitting your head on a brick wall. I'm getting nowhere.

Adviser: So maybe we could concentrate today on looking at what you are putting in your applications – and thinking of ways in which you could sound out employers about prospects before putting pen to paper.

When unemployment is prolonged, a person may lose sight of the fact that he has something valuable to offer an employer. Repeated rejections seem to confirm this view and the self-concept goes into a downward spiral. Unless this can be reversed, such an attitude is a serious depressant to both job prospects and the individual's mental outlook.

Case study: Stephanie

Friends said Stephanie was her own worst enemy in that she never gave herself credit for what she achieved. This personality trait was the main reason why she left school at the age of 16. Her employers would not have described her as a 'high flyer', but no one ever found her work less than totally satisfactory. Her last employer encouraged her to gain a Higher National Certificate (HNC) by day release, which she did more to satisfy him than for her own sake. To her surprise, she won a number of merit passes, but she had little concept of the value of these in the labour market.

Stephanie: It's really hard to stand out from the crowd when there are so many applicants. I have to be honest and say that most of the time I wouldn't choose me if I were an employer.

Adviser: You wouldn't choose you?

Stephanie: Well, what's a HNC when you can find folk with business degrees – and better work experience? I've only done odd bits and pieces of clerical and sales work – nothing very stretching.

Adviser:	You were able to hold down a job while simultaneously completing a part-time course successfully at the first attempt. Presumably that didn't just happen. There must have been some effort and skills involved there.
Stephanie:	Mmm ... I suppose so.
Adviser:	Perhaps you could list some of those skills so that we can see how to present your story to employers ... Maybe you have to help them to choose you!

An alternative reaction to despair may be anger, which can be equally counter-productive if it gets in the way of a job search. It can be difficult for a careers adviser to channel angry feelings in a more constructive direction. As the client speaks, it may feel as if the anger is directed at the adviser. It is important that the adviser should recognise the anger, try to understand where it is coming from and not react to it in the relationship.

Case study: Harry

Harry had left his last job more than a year previously on health grounds. Although still attending his doctor, he had been discharged as fit for work. His real remaining problem was his attitude at interviews. He was convinced that employers were out of line in asking him questions about his health and the circumstances of leaving his previous employment. He talked frequently of suing employers for prejudicial discrimination. Frequently, that anger seemed to overflow to encompass the careers adviser who was trying to help him with interview technique.

Harry:	I don't even know why I'm talking to you. It's been a waste of time coming here for the past six months.
Adviser:	You are feeling angry about another rejection ... I wonder if you are too angry to discuss your job interview as we had agreed?
Harry:	No, that's what I came for ... the interview was a total charade. It was all a fix. It was clear that the internal candidate would get the job. The rest of us were just a stage army. I've written to complain.
Adviser:	That was obviously a frustrating experience for you. You were hopeful of that job, I remember, and so I can understand your disappointment. Maybe

you needed to write that letter to get it out of your system.

Harry: Perhaps. I suppose it was a safety valve of some kind. But now I'm back to square one – no job and another unsuccessful interview to live down.

Adviser: We agreed at our last meeting that whatever the outcome of your interview, we could use it as a vehicle for measuring your progress with interview technique. I wonder if we could still use your recent interview experience constructively in this way ...

Sometimes in such situations a roleplay enables the client to hear how he comes across to others and to recognise his responsibility for the image which he is creating – whether it be lacking in confidence, disinterested or overly aggressive.

Case study: Anwar

Anwar had good qualifications and an excellent reference from school, but he felt very uncomfortable in interviews and came across as very shy and reserved. As a result most employers felt that he would have difficulty in fitting in with the rest of their workforce. After a run of unsuccessful interviews and pressure from home to do something positive, Anwar reluctantly agreed to let a careers adviser tape-record and play back a practice interview.

Adviser: Now that you have heard how you sound in an interview, I wonder how you would describe the impression which you give to others.

Anwar: A bit wishy-washy, really. Not very confident – which is true.

Adviser: What specific things gave you that impression?

Anwar: Well, I was very quiet – sometimes I could hardly hear the words ... my tone of voice was rather flat ... and the language sounded apologetic.

Adviser: I would agree with that. Now, let's think about how you could have transformed that impression by doing things differently. What would have been better?

Some clients may want to explore the possibility of unemployment being due to actual or imagined discrimination on grounds of gender, age, race, religion or disability. The challenge for the careers adviser in this situation is to acknowledge that such discrimination is a reality, but to enable the client to try to deal with it positively without being defensive.

Case study: Chloe

Chloe's sight had been deteriorating since she was in her twenties. She had adopted a very resilient attitude to this and had learned to make the most of her useful residual vision by learning to work with a computer with a closed circuit television (CCTV) enlarging facility. She reckoned that this, plus experience of working around offices all of her adult life ought to enable her to hold down a job as efficiently as any other worker. Many employers, however, did not appear to share her optimism and she was becoming increasingly frustrated about her job search.

Chloe: It is so galling to be called for interview and then spend most of the time talking about why they don't think I can do the job. They're not prepared to 'take the risk' with a visually impaired person – but I know I could do the jobs or I wouldn't have applied for them.

Adviser: So they are focusing on disability when you want to speak about your ability. That must be quite frustrating when you know full well that you could handle the work.

Chloe: Yes, it is. I'm sure that they don't spend as much time on what other candidates *cannot* do. They are so limited in their outlook that they cannot imagine that there are other ways of achieving the same end result.

Adviser: It sounds as if you could tell them a good deal about the methods which visually impaired people use in an office setting.

Chloe: Yes, and what's more, it wouldn't cost them anything because I have my own equipment.

Adviser: I'm getting the feeling that, while there may occasionally be outright discrimination, the problem may more often be due to the employers' lack of knowledge about how blind people work. I wonder how you could help them with that – perhaps even in advance of the interview.

Most unemployed clients do not expect to walk out of the careers interview with a job in their pocket. It is important, however, that the client should attain a positive sense of having been able to communicate with another person and to be understood in a non-judgemental way. This may be even more reassuring to the client than any positive actions which stem from the interview. Ideally, the client should also leave the interview with some thinking points to mull over and some actions to pursue.

Case study: Linda

Linda was making a gradual recovery from a debilitating illness and was worried about the gaps in her CV. She felt that she had to take steps to get 'a real job' as soon as possible and yet at the same time she was apprehensive about taking on more than she could handle at the risk of her health. In a careers interview she explained all the options and decided to follow her own inclinations.

Adviser: So, you've concluded that it is not wise to seek full-time employment until you are fully recovered from your illness. That makes a lot of sense. Maybe you could summarise how you see things now as a result of our discussion.

Linda: Yes. I realise that I don't have to feel guilty about not going back to work full-time. Nobody was pushing me to do so. That was a pressure coming from inside myself. Doing a good job part-time could be just as satisfying – and I could still have some energy left over for my own pleasure.

Adviser: That's right. There's no rule that says you have to wear yourself out on the job before you can relax. Maybe you would like to look now at how you could find suitable part-time work.

REDUNDANCY

Redundancy is an unwelcome situation which has faced many UK families. In manufacturing industries alone jobs have fallen by over 40 per cent between 1975 and 1995. In recent years similar exercises of radical reductions in the workforce have been carried out in financial organisations, the Civil Service and the armed forces – and the process continues.

The impact on a family's standard of living is bad enough when one family member loses a job, but in some instances of closures of businesses all adults in the family may be made redundant simultaneously, in which case the effect on income is catastrophic and the psychological impact on the family unit can be devastating.

People whose jobs are made redundant suffer all the same difficult feelings experienced by those who are unemployed for other reasons, but they are often exacerbated by additional complex sentiments, such as a sense of being betrayed, especially if they have worked overtime and accepted pay freezes or cuts in order to save their employer's organisation from bankruptcy or closure.

Once it becomes clear that redundancy is a fact, the initial phase of denial of the reality of the job loss may be replaced by powerful feelings of anger and bitterness. The emotions experienced at this stage are similar to those associated with bereavement. This is especially likely to be the case among people who have lost their jobs after years of loyal service to an organisation. Time-served tradespeople and experienced managers may never have had a day's unemployment in their lives and may require a scapegoat for the feelings of anger, shame, betrayal and disgrace which they may experience when made redundant.

In working with people who have been made redundant, a careers adviser should be aware of a number of factors which may be present. Unless these are brought out into the open and acknowledged, they can act as a block to future progress. The next two case studies show how these powerful emotions can emerge and be recognised in a careers interview.

Case study: Tom

Tom was a chargehand in a tractor factory, as was his father before him. In its heyday, the firm's name was synonymous with all that was good about British craftsmanship. Latterly, however, its products were undercut in the export market by manufacturers from the Far East. As its market share receded, the company was taken over by a Japanese firm which transferred production to a subsidiary where labour costs were lower. The closure of the plant was a blow to the whole community.

Tom: When I think of the hours that we put in at the factory
          – rarely less than a fifty hour week, sometimes more.
          And latterly we accepted a pay cut. .... And where did
          it get us? Nowhere. Out on my ear after twenty-three
          years – and not even as much as 'You did a good job,
          Tom'.

Adviser: It's hard to take, isn't it? I bet you're angry ... but I
          think you may be hurt as well?

Tom: That's right. It makes my whole working life seem of
          no account. I was really proud of our unit. When we
          won the Queen's Award for Exports ... we got a bonus
          that year, but it was the sense of being the best that
          mattered most.

Adviser: When you feel so rejected you can easily forget all that
          you have to offer. You are still the same person who
          did that. No one can take that away from you.

Tom: I know that on one level – but it's hard to feel like
          that at the moment.

Adviser: Yes, it's hard to take stock of your assets when you
          feel that you've been abandoned without a word of
          thanks. And yet it's important to do that if you are to
          go forward from here. Do you think we could begin
          to tackle that?

Case study: Barry

Had it not been for local government reorganisation, Barry might
have expected to continue in his workstudy job until retirement.
He had never been bothered about the fact that he could have
earned high wages in commercial consultancy, but he had prized
the apparent security of his job with the council – yet now nothing
seemed secure and he was pitch-forked into a new situation in
his fifties.

Barry: To be made redundant at 52 was certainly not in my
          game plan. My older son is at university and I have
          two other children still at school. An employment
          agency reckons it can get me occasional short-term
          contracts as a workstudy consultant, but it is likely to
          be sporadic ... and it's no use in pension terms. Right
          now, I feel in a panic about the situation. I don't know
          how we'll cope.

Adviser: Of course you feel in a panic. You have been with the council a long time and no doubt your job seemed secure until they contracted out management services and your job became redundant. Your feelings are entirely natural at a time like this.

Barry: I suppose it takes time to come to terms with the unexpected. It's a new ball game, wondering where your next wage is going to come from.

Adviser: Yes, it is. But perhaps you are already beginning to think of ways to avoid being entirely dependent on what the agency finds for you. Maybe you have contacts ...

Barry: Yes, I had thought about sending a batch of speculative letters. The fellow at the agency is very helpful, but he is not a specialist in my field. I reckon I have a fair idea of who might be interested in my type of expertise. It would do no harm to approach them. Apart from that, Jim McCormack, one of my former colleagues, had a notion about us setting up in business. I would never have contemplated that before, but I might think about it now.

Where whole communities have suffered a works closure, there may be a breaking up of families and circles of friends as young people and others who feel obliged to relocate in order to make a fresh start move away from the area. For both those who leave and those who remain this may have the effect of a double bereavement resulting in a period of traumatic readjustment, with major impacts on levels of self-confidence. This can be seen in the case of Gregor.

Case study: Gregor

Gregor had been well paid for his age in a technical post in a nuclear processing plant in a remote part of Scotland. The plant had been the major employer in the area, and when it was de-activated there was no work of a remotely similar nature for a young person with Gregor's qualifications. Influenced by his father, he moved to the central belt of Scotland, where he found a well-paid post in the computer manufacturing industry. Cut off from his friends and feeling conspicuous as a result of his different accent, he found it hard to control homesickness and nostalgia for a past which could not be re-created.

Gregor: I don't think I did the right thing. My dad said, 'Go. There's nothing left here.' I suppose I was lucky to get this job as a technician, but I hate living here. I'm cut off from all my friends – and folk here just aren't the same.

Adviser: It's hard when everything in your life is turned upside down all at once. New job, new location, new people. It's a lot to handle. I expect you feel pretty dis-orientated?

Gregor: Maybe I'll pack this job in and go back home.

Adviser: I wonder what would actually happen if you did that?

Gregor: I would feel more like myself at home. Not much prospect of a job, though. But I would be back with my friends – that is, the ones who are still there.

Adviser: So some things would be better – but some would be worse. It sounds too as if even home is not quite the same any more now that some of your friends have also moved away. I wonder if you can imagine how you might feel if you were to go home now?

Gregor: Great at first ... but I suppose I might get fed up hanging around with no job and no money – which was beginning to happen before. I don't know which is the lesser of two evils.

Adviser: Sounds like a difficult decision ... Mmm, I wonder how other folk are coping who also had to move away?

Gregor: I've been in touch with one or two. Danny seems to be making a go of it. He was in our football team and he's involved in sport where he is now.

Adviser: Mmm. A good way of meeting people with similar interests. Could there be any mileage in that approach for you ...?

UNDER-EMPLOYMENT

Much has been written about unemployment and redundancy, but little is said about under-employment. This term can be defined as employment of a type which does not fully utilise an indi-vidual's talents and intelligence and as a consequence is regarded as unfulfilling and depressing.

Many people may find themselves in this situation – school leavers on the poorer kind of work placement schemes, new graduates filling in with stop-gap jobs, returners to the labour market who cannot find work commensurate with their qualifications, people with disabilities and older workers whose experience may be disregarded and who are viewed as not capable of benefiting from further training.

If the period of time spent in such employment is protracted, it can be viewed by prospective employers and indeed by the job-holder herself as a block to entry to higher-level employment. The employer sees no evidence of greater capabilities because of the under-employment and the job-holder too may begin to harbour self-doubt about being able to cope with more demanding work once her confidence begins to slip.

Case study: Flora

The escalating costs of keeping two teenagers brought Flora into the labour market in a serious way. If truth be told, she was also looking for something to satisfy her need to be useful now that the children were spending less time at home. She had almost forgotten the ambitions which she had once cherished to make a career in the caring professions. Somehow she had been side-tracked from that. Was it too late to start now?

Flora: I had a degree once, but after the children went to school I just did whatever fitted in with their school hours – shop jobs, opinion polls – a few bits and pieces like that. I suppose I burned my boats really. Not much hope now of getting something more stimulating, is there?

Adviser: You say that you 'had a degree once' – but you still have it. That remains a symbol of your level of intelligence and achievement. And what about your 'bits and pieces' of work? Opinion polls, for instance. Presumably you had responsibility there – and you probably learned some new skills.

Flora: You have to be trustworthy . . . and tactful. You need stamina too . . . yes, and I suppose resilience in order to bounce back from rebuffs.

Adviser: I notice you say, 'You need . . .' – but we are actually talking about yourself. I guess you possess all these qualities, and it is these you can legitimately present to an employer as evidence of your potential to do a more demanding job. How do you feel about doing that?

Flora: A bit hesitant ... and yet I recognise what you are saying.

Adviser: If you can accept that, then maybe we can look at other skills acquired through your degree, your work experience and your time raising your family and see how these might translate into applications for work.

SUMMARY

This chapter has looked at some of the changes which are transforming the workplace in developed economies at the end of the twentieth century.

All of these trends in the labour market are normally beyond the control of an individual worker. This can lead to a sense of frustration if individuals feel that they are being manipulated by a system which they cannot influence; and the sense of helplessness can also lead to lowered self-esteem and passivity.

When there is no other outlet for these feelings, it can be useful for a client to voice them to a guidance practitioner. Having heard and understood the client's point of view, the guidance practitioner can help the client to move on from a perception of self as a victim of the system to a realisation that an individual, while not always able to choose her circumstances, always has a choice of a range of responses to those circumstances, and therefore some measure of control over the outcome, even when aspects of the situation are extremely challenging.

In the following brief chapter we shall look at the 'tools' now available in careers guidance, before moving on in Chapter 10 to consider the context of a single individual and the way the skills, and tools, are used with her in a verbatim account of her careers advisory interview.

Chapter 9

Tools available to the careers adviser

In this chapter we examine the current range of tools available to the careers adviser and where and how they can be most effectively introduced into the model. The tools we consider are:

- pencil and paper exercises;
- card sorts;
- computer-aided guidance systems (CAGS);
- psychometric instruments;
- interview role play;
- contacts with employers (work-shadowing and work experience);
- information services.

The adviser can learn to maintain the cooperative nature of the process and still nurture the developing empathy while introducing an appropriate tool. The danger for the adviser lies in reverting, in the eyes of the client, to being the 'expert' who will solve the problems, thus reinforcing client passivity. It is easy to produce one of these instruments like a rabbit out of a hat and give the impression that this will produce a magical answer. The timing of such interventions is vital. At the clarifying and exploring stages of this model the client is being encouraged to work together with the adviser, becoming actively involved in the process of the interview. The adviser may briefly mention that there may be tasks and exercises which could help in the process, but not at this stage. For most of these tools (there are some exceptions), the optimum time for introduction is during the evaluation and action-planning stages. At this point the adviser will:

- involve the client in the decision making about whether this would be a useful strategy to help her;
- allow the time to provide a proper explanation of the purpose and nature of the instrument selected;
- affirm, where necessary, that the adviser will offer appropriate interpretation and feedback.

The adviser uses his professional skills to decide on the most appropriate instrument(s). Care must be taken, however, not to confuse or demotivate the client by suggesting the use of too many of these tools at one time. Few careers advisers, in any case, have the time or resources to set a client a battery of tests, interest and personality questionnaires. The adviser must make careful decisions based on his perceived needs of the client and the objectives which the instrument can fulfil. The wrong tool is a waste of everyone's time.

When considering how to help the client to move forward, the adviser should clarify the objectives of introducing a tool, explore the instruments which are available, evaluate their effectiveness, and decide which one is appropriate and when and how to introduce it. Much of this assessment is completed internally but can be shared with the client, thereby enhancing the cooperative nature of the interview. The adviser will check out the client's previous experiences of such instruments, as a badly managed experience in the past can in some cases adversely affect the client's attitude and is a vital factor in deciding whether to use such tools.

PENCIL AND PAPER EXERCISES

There are several excellent interactive worksheets available, e.g. the Association of Graduate Careers Advisory Service's (AGCAS), 'Where Next?' and 'Know Yourself, Know Your Future', which encourage a client to reflect on what is important to him. Worksheets are an excellent strategy to move a client forward in self-awareness but they should be utilised outside the interview situation and brought back for discussion at another time. At the clarifying or exploring stages, it may be appropriate to point out the existence of worksheets to the client as a possible part of the action-planning stage. For example:

Adviser: Yes, it can be difficult to be clear about the range of skills you have developed through your work experience.

There is a worksheet available which could help you to do this. We can talk about it in more depth later, once you've had time to think it through for yourself.

CARD SORTS (e.g. SKILLS AND VALUES)

Some clients have difficulty in understanding the importance of identifying the skills they have or the value systems which they are operating. Others may find difficulty in verbalising these. Card sorts can be used to aid these processes. The client is asked to sort a number of cards, each describing a particular skill or value, into, for instance, their order of importance to the client. Cards, for example those produced by Lifeskills Associates, can be used effectively at an early point in the interview. By their nature, card sorts can be used interactively with the adviser. For example, the client can be encouraged to speculate out loud about the placing of individual cards to prioritise skills or values, which can offer an opportunity for effective challenging. This is a tool which can facilitate the cooperative nature of the interview. There are potential drawbacks – the client can more easily focus on the task and avoid any feelings associated with the issue concerned. The adviser will closely observe what is happening and draw the client back to her feelings if appropriate. Used effectively, however, such tools can aid the acknowledgement and exploration of some of the real issues for the client. Card sorts can equally be introduced at the action-planning stage. The client will often benefit from reflecting over a period of time on the relative importance of a range of skills and values.

COMPUTER-AIDED GUIDANCE SYSTEMS (CAGS)

A large range of CAGS is currently in use – e.g. PROSPECT, JIIG-CAL, CASCAID, GRADSCOPE, MICRODOORS, etc. They vary in their effectiveness for different clients at different times, but we are here concerned with how and when such tools can be most effectively used in the helping process. The client is actively involved in exploring the relative importance of factors in a structured manner and they can be used to help the client to see himself more objectively. The adviser will probably begin to identify an appropriate system fairly early in the interview during the clarifying phase at the point of making the initial assessment of the client's vocational maturity. CAGS can be particularly useful where:

- the client finds it difficult to talk about himself;
- the client has no ideas and needs to get started;
- the client seems to be resisting getting involved in the process (but see also below);
- the client has fixed ideas or prejudices which are not based on reality;
- the client has very limited job knowledge.

When such tools are introduced at too early a stage in the process, the counselling relationship will suffer. This happens when:

- the adviser is seen as the expert who can come up with the answers through the CAGS;
- the client is resistant to getting involved and his passivity may be reinforced;
- the adviser uses the CAGS to escape from an uncomfortable situation in the interview. This occurs most often in an adviser's early experience, but many practising advisers will recognise the temptation!

The ideal situation is where the system is available to the client and adviser on-line in the adviser's room so that it can be integrated smoothly and appropriately into the interview process. Not all advisers have this level of provision available. Experienced advisers will explore different methods of introducing CAGS so they can be integrated into the counselling model – e.g. in group work, or by encouraging clients to use a system before the interview to provide a basis for discussion.

CAGS cannot stand alone. They can facilitate the client's ability to continue the process started in the interview, but require interpretation from a skilled adviser. The client who has misplaced beliefs about both self and the process can feel bewildered by this task. If the resulting CAGS analysis comes as a bit of a shock – possibly no jobs appearing on the screen or a list of unrelated, really impractical suggestions – then intervention by a skilled adviser can help the client to challenge himself so that more realistic use can be made of the system.

One of the major benefits of CAGS to the adviser is this opportunity to challenge a client on his perceptions of himself in relation to the world of work. CAGS will often highlight inconsistencies in what the client is saying. For instance:

Adviser: Yes. The list of jobs you have produced does seem a bit odd. I wonder how the machine got here ... When we look at your responses, you say being able to develop your leadership skills is very important to you. You also say you prefer to work on your own. To me, that seems rather contradictory. How do you see it?

In summary, a CAGS can be incorporated in the counselling model in a variety of ways. The adviser will consider it during the clarifying stage. It may be mentioned at an early point, e.g. during the exploration stage, and can be built into the action-planning stage. CAGS is a tool for the adviser and the subsequent discussion can be very fruitful in enabling the adviser to utilise effective challenging in an objective way. CAGS is not normally helpful as a response to an unsatisfactory guidance interview.

PSYCHOMETRIC INSTRUMENTS (APTITUDE TESTS AND PERSONALITY QUESTIONNAIRES)

Aptitude Tests

Aptitude tests set out to measure a client's specific ability in a particular area at that particular time. They are especially useful:

- where the client is unrealistic (over- or under-confident) about the level of her ability;
- where the client wants to get some experience of the kinds of tests employers use in selection;
- where the client is confused about the level of ability she has in a particular area – e.g. a mature student who failed maths exams at school but who worked in an accounts office for many years.

A careers adviser is not able to predict how any one employer will use aptitude tests. This can lead to confusion for the client. The 'pass' mark for the same test used by a number of employers will be set at different levels. Some employers use tests as a means of pre-selection, others not until the final interview stage where the test results are only part of the selection process. The adviser introducing a test will explain very clearly the purpose of the test and what the client will gain from undertaking it.

Adviser: You seem unsure about how well you can manipulate numbers. This test will help you to be clearer about any difficulties you may have and we can then discuss how you could begin to tackle these.

The inherent danger in using tests is the risk of destroying the client's self-confidence if the test is set at an inappropriate level. The experienced adviser will be familiar with a range of tests and be able to select effectively. Using the counselling model in a subsequent feedback session will allow the adviser to challenge the client if necessary.

Personality questionnaires

Personality questionnaires, on the other hand, are more subjective and, like CAGS, a reflection of how a client sees herself. They involve helping the client to look more objectively at herself in relation to different types of jobs and are particularly useful where:

- a client is trying to decide between two or three types of work;
- a client has had considerable work experience and needs to stand back from considering the tasks involved to review how she works with people, her thinking style and her emotional balance;
- a client wants to gain experience of completing such a questionnaire;
- a client wants to prepare for a selection interview by determining what an employer might probe.

The adviser will introduce the possibility of completing a personality questionnaire at the action-planning stage, and will emphasise that this is a self-report which might give some clues about the way a client likes to work.

Both tests and questionnaires can be a useful aid to the careers adviser who wants to challenge inconsistencies in what the client is saying and doing, enabling her to make a more realistic assessment of the issue for herself. Once again, careful interpretation and feedback are essential. It is important to check how the client was feeling as she completed the paperwork. The adviser might want to know if she was ill, had just had an argument at home, or if there had been a recent criticism of her performance at work.

INTERVIEW ROLE PLAY

This is potentially a very powerful tool and is particularly useful where:

- the client wants to prepare for an impending interview;
- the client has consistently failed to achieve a job offer following interview and needs to diagnose what is going wrong;
- the client significantly lacks confidence, underestimates his ability, or is over-confident.

The practice interview provides real evidence of behaviour which allows the adviser to use immediacy and challenging skills effectively. This tool can be offered in a variety of formats depending on the needs of the client and the circumstances and setting of the environment in which the counselling interview takes place.

Methods

Brief practice interview questions as part of the counselling interview

As the counselling interview develops, it may emerge that the client has particular concerns over one type/style or topic of interview question. In order to help the client address this concern, or to assess if it is an appropriate concern, the adviser may challenge the client to try to answer such a question, without really getting into the role.

Adviser: You have mentioned several times that you are worried about how you will respond when employers ask about your epilepsy. Let's try it out now where we can think about it afterwards. What if I tried asking you the question, 'How does your epilepsy affect your daily life?'

John: It shouldn't affect it at all. I just need to be left alone after a fit. The problem is with other people who can't cope with it.

Adviser: The *words* you use make sense. Perhaps I could share with you what I observed when you said it, though. Your tone of voice sounds really angry – almost defiant. And the way you are sitting – arms crossed – makes me feel you are not prepared to discuss it. That's not very helpful if the employer is trying to work out if you will fit in to the organisation. Would you like to have another go?

This provides the client with the opportunity to try out various responses in a safe environment and could have the effect of reducing the anxiety connected with the question. The adviser can then use the skills at the higher level of the skills pyramid to enhance the client's self-awareness.

One-to-one practice interviews

It is not normally possible to integrate this into an advisory interview, and it would usually be arranged as a separate session. The process will fill one interview slot for the adviser. As a framework for the practice interview, the adviser should adhere to the interview model – clarifying, exploring, evaluating and action planning. There is a need to clarify with the client the purpose and the method of the role play. It can be helpful if the client is encouraged to raise issues which make him anxious at this stage, e.g. questions about the lack of relevant work experience or questions about a gap in work history.

The practice interview must be clearly a role play, a 'game' that is entered cooperatively. When the practice interview is taking place, the adviser adopts a different interviewing style – more probing, questioning, taking control. To emphasise the difference, it can be valuable to change the physical arrangements, e.g. move from low easy chairs to upright chairs or sit at a desk. The adviser will take notes – both to provide appropriate feedback and to simulate the selection interview situation. Once this stage is completed, the client and adviser will return physically to the original arrangement, enabling the transition back to the counselling mode. Once into the evaluating stage the adviser has a prime opportunity to challenge and to use immediacy, based on the empathy developed in the clarifying stage. The action-planning stage enables the client to decide how to act on the feedback given.

In this example session, the adviser is probing some of what emerged in the practice interview.

Adviser: You said you thought you didn't come over in a positive way. At which points in the interview do you think this happened?

Hilary: I suppose when I mentioned not getting on with one of my previous employers.

Adviser: I agree you didn't sound positive then. I wasn't sure why you raised it at first – and you brought it up later in the interview.

Hilary: Well, you asked . . . [Pause]. No, maybe you didn't ask about that specifically. You wanted to know why I am interested in *this* job.

Adviser: That's right. And until you mentioned it I had no idea (as the selector) that you had problems getting on with that employer. Then you mentioned it again later. I wonder if we could work out what was going on.

Hilary: You know I'm very worried that it could happen again. Maybe that means I feel I have to mention it.

As a result of the practice interview, the adviser now has the opportunity to explore with the client the nature of the difficult relationship with a previous employer and to consider how this is affecting performance at interview.

Using video recording/playback for feedback

This involves expensive equipment, but is available to some careers advisers. It is also potentially expensive in the use of time, and the adviser must develop some skill in its effective use. It is, however, an extremely powerful tool. The adviser takes the role of selector and interviews the client for the job he is applying for. The 'interview' or short section of the 'interview' is taped on video, then played back to the client, who can often immediately see for himself how his behaviour could be interpreted by a selector. Where time permits, the client can rehearse responses to difficult questions and try them out again. For some clients, considerable trust must develop before they are prepared to face the camera and it is vital that the adviser utilises her counselling skills to foster trust to get started and to provide the most effective feedback afterwards. This tool is often used with small groups as an extremely effective way of using time and resources, as clients learn a great deal from observing and giving feedback to others. The adviser must control the session firmly and model appropriate feedback – both positive and negative. Some individuals may require one-to-one time with the adviser soon after the session to clarify and reinforce their learning in a supportive manner.

CONTACTS WITH EMPLOYERS

An effective careers adviser develops a network of employer contacts, both formally and informally. One of the best ways for a client to test out different types of work is through first-hand experience, which can be done through:

- work-shadowing;
- short career 'taster' courses;
- work experience;
- local contacts prepared to talk to clients.

The availability of such tools depends on the work environment of the adviser. School and higher education careers advisers tend to have strong networks of employers prepared to be involved in this way. To make this tool more effective, there are several principles which the adviser must bear in mind:

1 The employer must be carefully briefed about the needs of the client and the level of work which is appropriate.
2 The client should be properly prepared for the experience. She should be aware of the expectations of the employer in terms of conduct and dress. It is essential that the client identifies what she is hoping to achieve through the experience, and takes time to assess the outcome.
3 The client should be carefully debriefed following the experience. Gentle probing by the adviser will enable the client to get the most out of the experience, by reflecting on it to weigh up the pros and cons of that type of work and that kind of working environment and so enable her to move along the career-planning process.

INFORMATION SERVICES

The provision of information has already been closely examined in Chapter 5. It is, however, appropriate in this chapter to outline the range of information to which the careers adviser has access. Currently there is a vast explosion of information in society – no less so in the careers world. In addition to conventional written information, the adviser can draw on computer-generated information and video material. Experienced advisers also hold information gleaned from visits to employers and contact with other clients which may be of value. There are three guiding principles for the adviser in providing information sources for the client:

1 The information must be accurate and up to date.
2 The information must be provided at a level which is appropriate for the individual client.
3 The information must be accessible to the client.

SUMMARY

In summary, the general points the adviser should bear in mind when planning to introduce some of the tools described in this chapter include:

- introducing the tool at an appropriate stage in the interview process;
- explaining the nature and purpose of the tool and how it fits in to the process;
- checking the client's previous experience of such tools;
- involving the client in the process of selection of the tool;
- ensuring the tool is at a level appropriate to the client;
- providing effective feedback and analysis of the tool;
- involving the client in the analysis;
- limiting the number of tools used at any one time.

Chapter 10

Carol: the context of guidance and the guidance interview

This chapter provides the opportunity to examine in depth the case history and recent guidance intervention for one client, Carol.

Carol is not a real person, but the details below are drawn from the realities of the work of careers advisers with numerous clients. The experienced adviser will no doubt recognise some of the circumstances and dilemmas which Carol presents. The first part of the chapter outlines the sociological context, the family history and its effects and Carol's experiences of guidance at different stages of her development. It then goes on to demonstrate, through a record of the dialogue during the careers advisory interview, how the adviser works with the fears and expectations which Carol is carrying and the specific ways in which the adviser uses herself to interact and enable Carol to move forward.

CAROL'S CONTEXT

Carol is a member of a working-class family in a sector of society where the male parent was traditionally expected to provide for the family and the female parent's role was child rearing. Little contact was made outside this social grouping. A daughter's role was to marry early and continue the traditional pattern. Paid work for girls was necessary between school and marriage, but the concept of a 'career' for a girl in this sociological context was alien.

As Carol was growing up during the 1970s, a great many pressures developed on the family unit which disturbed the traditional pattern and initiated change. The economic pressures of declining manufacturing industry and rapid inflationary increases resulted in the loss of many traditional jobs. With their men out of work, many women found themselves in the job market and working to provide for the family. At the same time (and perhaps partly as a result of this) women in other sectors of society were actively questioning their traditional role. The rapid increase in opportunities in higher education during the 1960s had produced women with high expectations of career prospects, although most women still assumed the child rearing role and withdrew from the job market once children were born. Educational qualifications began to have greater importance in job opportunities.

Within the traditional working-class family unit, these pressures produced disturbance of the long-established roles and relationships. All family members experienced insecurity. The male parent's right to be consulted on all decisions was undermined and the female parent experienced the burden of responsibility for providing for the family. Economic pressures hit hard, as unemployment took its toll and the increased availability of consumer goods encouraged many to get into debt.

These sociological changes influenced the developing value systems of young people like Carol. There was a great deal of uncertainty emerging about their future role. They experienced changing role models within the family; while some grasped the changes as opportunities, others were threatened by the lack of a clear path for the future. Changing relationships within the family also disturbed the potential relationships to be made outside the family unit; for example, relationships with the opposite sex and relationships with authority figures.

It was in this context that Carol grew up, and her family history reflects the socio-economic pressures of the time.

CAROL'S FAMILY HISTORY

When Carol first came to the Careers Service, she was 26 years old, single, the youngest (by five years) of three sisters. She had just completed a degree in sociology and was at the point of moving into the next phase of her life.

She is the daughter of working-class parents in a traditional family where father earned the living and mother stayed at home to bring up the children. Father's rule was law and he was consulted on all decisions. As the girls grew older, the mother was keen to take some part-time work to get out of the house and earn some extra cash. Father was very much against this and withheld his permission (without which mother would not work) for several years. Eventually, when Carol was almost 12 years old, her mother started work in a local supermarket. The two older sisters had left school and had started work as typists locally. Father was a miner and at this time there were threats of redundancy in the Coal Board. There was a great deal of uncertainty around. This uncertainty, followed some months later by his redundancy, caused great disruption to the long-established relationships within the family. Mother became the family breadwinner, with contributions from the older sisters. Carol's father, unemployed for two years, became very depressed. It became even more important to him to be able to control the lives of his family, who began to see their firm but caring husband and father as an irrational bully with an easily aroused temper. Carol's mother was anxious and resentful at the responsibilities she had been forced to take on. The relationships which had functioned well enough before were now damaged and neither parent seemed able to discuss what was happening. There was constant anxiety about money. In the process of all this, Carol entered adolescence lacking the care and attention she had previously enjoyed (her parents were now too wrapped up in their own problems). She became sullen and angry. Her school work deteriorated and she began to stay out late at night.

After two years, Carol's father found regular work. While the parents' relationship had changed permanently, they nevertheless settled into a marriage more like that of their earlier years. Carol continued to rebel. She began to despise her mother for 'giving in' to her father. The life ambitions of her two sisters appeared to be satisfied as they made early marriages and gave up work to have children. Carol was led to understand that this was what her parents expected of her. Her school work produced disappointing results. She did not see any point in it and left school at the earliest opportunity, refusing to visit the careers officer. Unable to gain permanent employment (as a result of poor academic results and a declining job market), Carol drifted through a number of temporary jobs: sales work, waitressing and bar work. She was prepared to put in the effort as required, but the purpose of the work was to earn the money to enjoy herself. At the age of 18 she was still living at home, increasingly at loggerheads with her father. As she drifted through a series of jobs, so she drifted in and out of a series of relationships, reluctant to commit herself for too long to any one boyfriend. There was one who made it clear he wanted a long-term relationship, but she refused to let herself become involved and felt she had hurt him badly. Gradually her circle of friends moved on to college or university, to marriage or to work elsewhere. She began to feel increasingly isolated both within her family and outside. She was unsettled and disappointed with life. It was also becoming increasingly difficult to maintain her work pattern. Employers were keen to take younger and therefore cheaper school leavers to do the work she was used to. She began to talk about moving to the city.

A chance meeting with her former school history teacher made her look at other options. History was the one subject she had enjoyed at school – as much to do with the approach of this particular teacher as the nature of the subject. The teacher was now working in the local college and, slightly provocatively, suggested Carol should come to his evening class. She had part-time work in a shop, had just broken up with her latest boyfriend and her closest friend had recently left the town to go to college. Carol could see a long winter ahead of her, so decided she had 'nothing to lose' by going to the history class.

In spite of her initial reservations, she soon began to enjoy it enormously. It provided a focus for her week. She could retreat into a history book at home and looked forward to the class discussions. Several of the class were applying that year (as mature students) for university courses. Their talk of choosing subjects and universities made Carol realise that she too could take decisions about her life. A university degree could provide the opportunity to move away from home and the constant referrals to 'settling down', and enable her to meet more of the kind of people she knew through her history class. She signed up for further classes in the following year and planned to apply to university after that.

Her mother proved an unexpected ally. Her own life experiences had made her aware of how she had suppressed her own somewhat limited ambitions to the needs and expectations of her husband and family. She encouraged Carol to take the opportunities she could see before her. For the first time Carol felt she could relate to her mother. At this point, Carol's ambition did not stretch beyond getting into university with the hope of getting a degree. She had limited experience of the world of employment, none of postgraduate work, and was indeed far from ready to look that far ahead. There were so many hurdles facing her at that moment and as her exams approached she became less convinced that she would achieve the necessary grades. However, she did better than expected and was admitted to the university of her first choice at the age of 22.

She had registered to study history as her main subject, but was required to choose two other subjects to study in her first year. She made this choice almost at random, selecting subjects she had not taken at school without really knowing anything about them.

Carol spent much of her first year in acute anxiety. She felt so much older than the majority of new students, many of whom appeared so much more confident and clever than she. She constantly felt 'someone' would find out she was not good enough to be there and would ask her to leave. Her first written work assessments, however, gave her greater confidence and she began to contribute in tutorials and to participate with enjoyment in the process of learning.

By the end of her first year she decided to change her main subject from history to sociology. There was a higher proportion of mature students in the sociology department and while she was able to work comfortably alongside the younger students, she enjoyed belonging to a group of more mature students. She also realised that she could draw on her life experience in her study of sociology.

The group of mature students she was close to were highly motivated academically. A few had already decided that they wanted an academic career and this became the aim of the group as a whole. Carol was swept along with this, partly because she had no knowledge or experience of alternative options, but also because she felt she belonged in the group. She felt she had grown away from her family and friends at home and felt increasingly isolated when she returned home.

She had formed an intimate relationship with one particular student and had allowed herself to become more emotionally involved than ever before. He, too, was sitting his final exams that summer. Whether the pressure of study had been too great, or the relationship was ready to end in any case, Carol was devastated when they separated two weeks before her exams. This probably contributed to her award of a lower-second degree rather than the upper-second she required for the postgraduate funding for which she had applied. It was at this point that she approached the University Careers Service for the first time.

REFLECTIONS ON CAROL

We have seen that the influences on Carol's life pattern were varied. They were also, however, cumulative and developmental. Carol's family circumstances, including the relationship with her sisters and parents, her experiences at school and work, and the contacts and developing self-awareness achieved at university, had all contributed to her attitudes and value system at that stage in her life.

The acute change in lifestyle and family circumstances when her father was made redundant at the time of greatest personal emotional upheaval during adolescence had left her reluctant to form permanent relationships with the opposite sex and with a real fear of allowing someone else to control what happened to her. Her rebellion in her teenage years denied her the academic opportunities she might have enjoyed on leaving school. The limited expectations of family reinforced this. As she moved out of adolescence into an adult stage, she realised how isolated she had become through her behaviours. It was only a chance meeting with the history teacher that began to open options. Appropriate intervention by a careers officer then enabled her to make an assessment of who she was and who she wanted to become. Carol's story is a demonstration of some of the psychological, sociological and also chance influences on an individual's career path. Thus, it is in this context that we can see the intervention of a careers adviser as part of a process, but in no way can it be the end of that process.

CAROL'S EXPERIENCE OF GUIDANCE

Carol's first experience of careers guidance had been at the point of choosing school subjects. An appointment had been made with the careers officer at school and her parents were invited. Her mother was working and unable to attend, and so her father came to the school. There had been a blazing row that morning about her late nights and deteriorating school results. While the careers officer worked hard to draw Carol out, she was uncooperative and sullen. Feeling she had no control over what the adults wanted her to do, she shrugged her shoulders in helpless compliance and followed a similar course to her sisters. She left the interview feeling angry and resentful. The careers officer had offered the opportunity for further meetings as it was clear to her that Carol had not participated in the decision making, but Carol had insisted on seeing her as just another controlling adult. When on leaving school Carol received an invitation to attend the careers office, she remembered vividly her earlier experience and refused to go.

Later, when she began to get good marks for her written work during her evening class, Carol took advice from one of the other students and made an appointment to see the careers officer attached to the college. She could remember clearly her first experience of guidance and so was initially very wary and arrived with a list of questions, seeking information about further study. This time, she was prepared to listen and the adviser gently encouraged her to explore her motivation for further study and to consider what she wanted out of her life generally. Carol was just beginning to become more open to the guidance process.

CAROL'S CURRENT FEARS AND EXPECTATIONS

When Carol approached her University Careers Service for the first time, she was, however, still carrying certain fears and expectations from her past. She had already graduated, but far from being happy about her achievements, Carol was disappointed in her results, which in her eyes were holding her back from what she believed she wanted to do. She had a sense of failure in this area of her life, and also in respect of her relationships. The separation from her partner at a crucial time had undermined her confidence. The only way forward seemed to be to fall back on the financial support of her family. She regarded this step as a blow to her independence and was anxious about the control which her father would regain. She felt defeated and strongly remembered a related feeling from long ago when she had first seen the careers officer at school. She was not yet aware of the ways in which these feelings could be influencing her career plans and decisions. In addition, the careers service had sent letters to all students early in their final year inviting them to make contact and Carol was uncomfortable that she had not responded then. She hoped the careers adviser would be able to suggest other sources of funding for the place on the course she had been offered which would maintain her independence from her family. She was reluctant to reveal much of the turmoil within her to a relative stranger.

SUMMARY OF THE INTERVIEW

The adviser picked up her initial anxiety at an early point in the interview and used the clarifying phase to explain what Carol could expect from her and what was expected of Carol. She resisted providing bare information in order to concentrate on developing empathy, thus allowing Carol to express some of her tentative feelings. Once the initial story had been told, the adviser moved into the exploring phase to clearly spell out what might be achieved in the time available and check out this 'contract' with Carol. As she began to explore the initial issues, the adviser became aware that other feelings were present – strong feelings of anger and bitterness. The empathy which had been developed allowed the adviser to gently probe these feelings and identify with Carol some of the areas which were painful for her: her disappointment at her results and the break-up of the relationship with her boyfriend. The adviser acknowledged the feelings and encouraged Carol to explore how these had influenced the decisions she had had to make.

Further exploration encouraged Carol to uncover her confusion over her relationship with her family, in particular with her father and her anxiety about losing control of her independence. The recognition of these as influencing factors enabled Carol to review more clearly the decisions she had to take and to begin to reflect realistically about the direction she had planned to take.

Towards the end of the exploring phase, the adviser examined for herself whether the initial contract required review or whether other issues had great importance. First she referred to the agreed contract in order to remind Carol of it and to move the interview forward.

During the evaluation phase, the adviser employed the skills of immediacy and challenging to enable Carol to prioritise what was most important for her in work, bearing in mind all the influencing factors raised earlier. She used the experiences Carol had already mentioned to help her identify her strengths in terms of interest and ability. The adviser then began to introduce some relevant information, but carefully avoided overloading Carol with details and suggested ways in which she could find out what she needed to know.

The interview, below, has been separated into the four phases of the model as the adviser works through it, but it is not evident from the dialogue that the adviser is moving from one phase to another. The progression seems natural and uncontrived.

The dialogue between Carol and her adviser is presented along with the internal dialogue (*in italics*) of the adviser in order to demonstrate what is going on in the process for the adviser.

You will remember that, as she arrived for the session, Carol still remembered her first encounter with an adviser at school and was not sure what to expect. Uppermost in her mind was the need to make a decision about the postgraduate course place she had been offered, without any funding. She was met in the reception area of the careers service by the careers adviser, whom she had never met before; nor had she ever visited the careers service in her time at university. The careers service had sent letters to all final-year students inviting them to make contact and Carol was uncomfortable that she had not responded, and wondered if the careers adviser would be cross . . .

THE CLARIFYING PHASE

Adviser: Hello Carol. My name is Lynda. We have about three-quarters of an hour together. This is your time, so perhaps you could tell me what you are hoping to get out of our discussion.

Carol: I hope I'm not wasting your time. I just want you to tell me if I should do this postgraduate course in Research Methods.

Adviser: (*She looks ready to run – sitting on the edge of her seat, very little eye contact. I wonder what her expectations of me are? My first tasks are to clarify our roles and to begin to build empathy.*)

No, you are not wasting my time. My role here is to help you work through the decision-making process for yourself. Would you like to tell me how you got to this point?

(*She's put her bag down and is sitting back a bit. Still very little eye contact, though perhaps she's beginning to relax.*)

Carol: Well, I don't see what else I can do. I've been offered a place. It's using my degree. I don't know much about anything else. I don't have a lot of contacts like a lot of people here. As for my degree – what use is a 2ii

in sociology? And I know mature students have difficulty finding jobs.

Adviser: (*I note she is plucking at her sleeve. This prickliness in
her manner may be hiding anxiety. She may need some
reassurance. My task is to build empathy and to
acknowledge her feelings. I must be wary of being drawn
into full-blown information provision at this point rather
than helping her face her anxiety.*)

You sound rather anxious as you say all that.

Carol: Yes, I am. [Sighs with relief.] My head is a real mess.
There's so much going on ... so many things to think
about. And I don't know what sort of work I'm suited
to, so the course might not be any use ...

Adviser: (*There is some eye contact now. There is a sense of relief
at having her feelings recognised but also something like
helplessness or confusion about the tasks ahead. I need
to understand what is behind her confusion before we
can build a contract.*)

It must all seem very confusing. Maybe we could
clarify some of the factors which are around for you.
For instance, what made you apply for this research
course?

Carol: Well, I wanted to use my degree. And I thought I
wanted to be an academic.

Adviser: It sounds as if you might not be quite sure now.

Carol: No, I'm not. For lots of reasons. Maybe I just drifted
into it.

Adviser: Can you say what it is about being an academic which
appealed to you?

Carol: Well, I suppose it's what I saw around me really. I could
see what the job involved. It seemed a logical progression. I enjoyed researching my dissertation. I'd like to
pass on my knowledge to others. But perhaps that's
not the only possibility?

Adviser: What other kinds of work did you consider?

Carol: Nothing very seriously, really. I didn't know where to
start. My experience before coming to university was
very limited – I just drifted from one temporary job to
another. I don't think I ever thought about work *after*
university.

Adviser: (*She is now a bit more relaxed in her seat, and we have
established good eye contact. She seems ready to work*

with me rather than waiting for me to produce a solution.
Her job knowledge seems limited and, so far, her self-
awareness still seems fairly superficial. My next task is to
develop an initial contract.)

THE EXPLORING PHASE

Adviser: Well, graduates in sociology do go on to do a wide
range of jobs and, later on, I can show you what our
graduates have done. Career choice is a process of
learning – learning about the nature of jobs and also
learning about ourselves. It's only when we have good
clear knowledge of both that we are in a position to
make effective decisions. It would be difficult for us to
cover all that in this time here. Perhaps we should
concentrate on what is important to you in a job and
see how that relates to the decision you have to make.
Does that seem a good use of our time?

Carol: Yes. But I don't know where to start.

Adviser: Well, you seem to be questioning the idea of an
academic career. Could you start by explaining what
your doubts are?

Carol   Will I really like it? Am I good enough? And [pause]
[slowly]:   is it worth all the risks?

Adviser: *(There are several factors here. I can work with one*
but must remember to pick up the others at a later
stage.)
Risks?

Carol: Yes, risks. To start with, there are the financial risks.
I've already got debts. Because I only got a 2ii, I've
been told that with limited funding I will not get a
grant. I know my exams went badly but I thought ...

Adviser: *(I'm feeling waves of emotion. Her voice has become*
very flat, she is looking down. Is it sadness she's trying
to hide or more like bitterness? I'm not sure yet.)
It sounds as if you were very disappointed with your
results.

Carol: It's hardly worth having, is it?

Adviser: What makes you say that?

Carol: I used to go round with all the other mature students
in the department. I really enjoyed the intellectual

arguments we had and liked being with people like myself. It was very important to all of them to get a really good degree. It was as if they wanted to prove something about mature students. I just got caught up in it all. It was an awful blow when I got the results.

Adviser: And you still have strong feelings about it?

Carol: It just seems so unfair! I broke up with my boyfriend just before the finals ... I'm sorry. You don't want to hear all this.

Adviser: (*Her disappointment is very strong. She is very distressed and tearful. She's not sure I'll accept her hurt and disappointment.*)

Well, take your time. I don't want to pry but it sounds as if it could be relevant to how you are feeling about the decision you have to make.

(*I must be wary of going too far down this road unless it proves really relevant. But it is clearly on the surface at the moment, so giving her the opportunity to talk about it briefly could move her forward.*)

Carol: Well, because of the break-up, I'm sure it affected my studying, so that's why I got such a poor class of degree. It's so unfair. It's all my fault.

Adviser: (*She sounds very much like an angry child who feels powerless.*)

You sound pretty angry – I wonder who you are angry with?

Carol: It's him. [Pause.] No, that's not fair either. We were both under pressure from exams. I suppose I was as much at fault, I may have pushed him into it. Actually, it looks as though we might get back together now all the pressure is off. I think I should share the blame. It was just unfortunate it happened then.

Adviser: (*I must be careful to continue to acknowledge her feelings and show that I accept them as real, rather than diving in to contradict her with more positive attitudes.*)

It sounds as if you were both under pressure and I think now you're having difficulty coming to terms with not getting a 2i.

Carol: Yes, that's right. People can say all they like about it being a good standard of degree from a good university, but I can't accept it for me.

Adviser: It sounds as if your head does know the facts but your heart denies it. I wonder what would help you to accept it?

Carol: I don't know.

Adviser: Take your time.

Carol: Perhaps one way would be if I got a decent job out of it. That would convince me a bit, I suppose.

Adviser: Most people with 2ii degrees do get good jobs and there is no reason to believe you will not. It sounds, though, that not getting funding for this course may be reinforcing for you the feeling that you have done badly, even if in reality you've done well enough.

Carol: [Heavy sigh.] That was the last straw when I heard about it yesterday.

Adviser: And yet you are still considering the course. How would you fund it?

Carol: I was hoping you would have some ideas but . . . [Long pause.] My father has offered to pay for it.

Adviser: That sounds very generous of him! .

Carol: Don't I know it! He will never let me forget it. He was not very keen for me to come to university in the first place. No one in our family ever did so before. My two sisters just did some nice clerical work, married nice men and now have a brood of nice children. They could never understand why I had to be different. Don't get me wrong – they were really proud when I graduated, but . . . I don't feel part of them any more. Now I'm just doing bar work, they are saying what a waste it all was if I don't get a good job. But Dad won't see me stuck – he's still got his redundancy money tucked away and that's what he's prepared to give me. But I don't know . . .

Adviser: (*There are some very confused emotions emerging here. She sounds really angry at the beginning of this explanation but towards the end I sense something else – wistfulness? I need to check it out.*)

You seem to have mixed emotions about accepting help from your father.

Carol: Yes. [Long silence.] I wish I didn't have to ask.

Adviser: You sounded quite angry just now.

Carol: There are always strings attached. Don't get me wrong.

They really are concerned about me. But, well, they think all this university nonsense has put strange ideas into my head ... [Long pause.] It would give him control over me again.

Adviser: Control?

Carol: I went to university to get away from all that. It was what *I* wanted to do. I was so sick of being told what was right and what was wrong (I was usually wrong). University was a way of being me.

Adviser: And you're afraid you might lose that if you accept his help.

Carol: Mmm. As I'm talking, I realise just how much I've moved away. I don't belong any more. [Pause.] I don't know where I belong.

Adviser: (*That sounds like the feeling of wistfulness I heard earlier.*)
Mmm. I think I understand that. I wonder if what you are feeling is a sense of loss?

Carol: Yes. In a way I feel lost.

Adviser: You've moved away from family to some extent, but you are also at another stage in life which involves change and movement.

Carol: You mean finishing my degree? I hadn't thought of it in that way. But yes. I had some good friends in the other mature students, but now they have all moved on. I seem to be stuck – in limbo.

Adviser: I wonder how that affects how you view the post-graduate course?

Carol: Maybe I'm trying to hold on to what I had. But it can't be the same, can it? The people will change ...

Adviser: Yes, moving on can be quite scary. Perhaps some of your confusion – you described it as 'my head is a mess' – comes from this fear of moving away from what you had and what you know.

Carol: Yes. That could be so. I realise I don't know where I belong any more. It's hard to let go, though. Maybe if I had a clearer idea of what job I am suited for I would find it easier.

Adviser: (*She is beginning to relate what she is discovering about herself to her sense of identity and how this fits with her views of jobs.*)

I expect you are 'suited to' a wide range of jobs –
most graduates are. Let's go back to what you were
saying earlier. We've talked about some of the risks
you can see if you do the course and we've identified
some of your reasoning in applying for it.

(*I now need to go back and pick up some of the
points she made earlier which could be significant.*)

I seem to remember you saying something about not
being sure if you would like it?

Carol: It does seem a very competitive world. I don't like that
sort of atmosphere. Also the academic world is very
rarified. And with my degree, realistically, I would find
it very hard to go beyond this MSc course.

Adviser: Realistically that's probably so. But let's concentrate
for now on what you would and would not like about
an academic career – that could give us clues about
other types of work you would enjoy.

(*It is safe now to be clearly realistic about her chances
in the academic field. Trust has developed and the
resulting empathy enables her to accept the reality. I'm
concerned about our time at this stage and how well we
are fulfilling the contract. It is necessary to draw her
back to this as I move into the evaluating phase.*)

THE EVALUATING PHASE

Carol: I know I would enjoy the research part of it – I put a
great deal into my dissertation, I got really involved in
it. Maybe it took too much of my time.

Adviser: Tell me more about that.

Carol: Well, I was researching how the advertising industry
influences what the consumer buys. It involved devising
a questionnaire, persuading people to fill it in and
making some sense of the results. Oh, and I went to
talk to a couple of advertising agencies as well.

Adviser: I can see you enjoyed doing it. Your face and voice
just light up when you are talking about it.

(*I can use immediacy in a positive way here.*)

Carol: Yes. Partly because it was something I did on my own
and I could see the results. Maybe you're going to tell
me I should go into advertising.

Adviser: (*She is grasping at job labels. My task is to help her identify her ideal job description at this point.*)
　　　　　We could look at that later, but I'm more interested at this point in analysing with you what you enjoyed in these tasks. We can think about job labels at a later stage. It sounds as if you liked the autonomy of doing your dissertation and also the practical nature of it.

Carol: Yes, that's so. But I wouldn't want to be working on my own all the time. I would like to work with people.

Adviser: In what way?

Carol: What do you mean?

Adviser: Well there are different ways of working with people. You could be helping people with their problems, or persuading them – to adopt your ideas or to buy something, for instance. You could be working in a team, or teaching people, or providing information . . .

Carol: I see. I don't want to be a social worker.

Adviser: (*We're back to putting labels on again. Perhaps I can use it to check out her concept of social work.*)
　　　　　No?

Carol: Well, they're just middle-class do-gooders – most of them have never had any real problems themselves and can't really understand what it's like. My parents would never accept it.

Adviser: (*We're back to parental control. She clearly has strong feelings about this, but may not realise how it is influencing her freedom of choice.*)
　　　　　Hmm. [Gently.] And it's important your parents can accept what you do?

Carol: Oh dear! That's interesting isn't it? I need to think about that.

Adviser: It *is* interesting – especially when we remember what you said before about moving away from your family. Perhaps you have still got some of their values which are important to you? We could come back to that later if you like.

Adviser: (*I have to make a decision about moving the interview on. She's become aware of the apparent inconsistency and probably needs time to consider it.*)
　　　　　In the meantime, let's see what we've got so far. You would like a job where you have some autonomy,

where you can see results and where you have contact with people. But we haven't yet defined what sort of contact, although 'helping' in terms of social work does not seem to be right.

Carol: Yes. And I wouldn't like to sell things, but I'm quite good at persuading people to do things.

Adviser: Tell me more about that.

Carol: Well, I was on the staff–student liaison committee. There was a real problem for some mature students with children to do with the timing of some of our tutorials. I managed to persuade the staff concerned to offer alternative tutorial times.

Adviser: So you were acting as an advocate for the others and were able to influence the attitudes of the staff?

Carol: It wasn't easy, but it was very satisfying to get a result.

Adviser: I wonder if you can see yourself doing this in a commercial setting?

Carol: Actually – I have thought about this one. I am really not interested in the profit motive. I want to be useful . . .

Adviser: Useful?

Carol: Well, doing something worthwhile. [Pause.] I suppose I should ask myself what I mean by that? [Pause for longer time.] It's got to make a difference in some way for the individual – I'm more interested in how what I do affects the individual than in measuring its value to the organisation. Does that make any sense?

Adviser: (*She is learning the process of self-analysis for herself now.*)

I think I understand. You want to work in a setting which provides a service for the individual, but not where that service is measured in cash terms.

Carol: Yes, that's right.

I think I want to work in the public sector. [Pause.] What about *your* job?

Adviser: (*I wonder what is happening now? There are a number of possibilities. She could genuinely have realised that what is happening here is the kind of role she wants. Or strong empathy has developed – she is relating to me personally, not the job – e.g. she is enjoying being understood and wants me to like her more. Or she would like to be me.*

I must remember her feelings of loss and not belonging.

My task is to ascertain which possibility is happening and to move on from there. I must be wary of feeling flattered. It is important I take it seriously and try to understand her motives.)

We can certainly look at being a careers adviser. But I would be interested to know what prompted you to say that just now.

Carol: I don't know. It just seems interesting, I suppose.

Adviser: Go on.

Carol: Well, you are making me think about things that matter, and you're listening to me . . .

Adviser: And perhaps you feel that is worthwhile. Perhaps you need to sort out whether you find it interesting because of the tasks I am doing or because we seem to be on the same wavelength.

Carol: I see. Mmm. I realise it is a long time since I felt someone understood me. I think it is probably a mixture of both – but maybe I need to find out more about being a careers adviser before I make up my mind.

Adviser: (*I must be wary about being sidetracked from the main activity which is to clarify key factors important for her.*)

I can certainly help you to follow that up. We were trying to work on the factors which are important to you in a job – trying to draw up your ideal job description really. You seem to want to be in the public sector. What other factors are important?

Carol: Variety is important too. The bar work – and all those boring jobs I did before I came to university – well, maybe I was meeting all sorts of different people, but the jobs I had to do – just the same things over and over again. I don't want to know what every day will bring.

Adviser: OK. Can I take you back to something you said earlier? It was where you were talking about being part of the group of mature students and how much you enjoyed working together. I'm wondering how much you want to work with people in that way?

Carol: I think I need to have some contact with people who think in the same sort of way. But not necessarily all

	the time – I'd be satisfied if I was able to meet them sometime during the day.
Adviser:	We agreed earlier to try to identify what factors are important to you in a job and then to relate them to the decision you have to make. I think we've come a long way in the first part. Perhaps you could summarise where we have reached.
Carol:	OK. Well, something in the public sector, where I can see results, have some autonomy. Variety is important, and something worthwhile – providing a service to the individual in the real world. And where I can see some prospects.
Adviser:	*(She seems clearer now about what she wants. This is a good point at which to take her back to the decision about the postgraduate course.)*
	So how do you think that would be satisfied if you did the postgraduate course?
Carol:	I hadn't thought of it in that way ...
Adviser:	Have a go now.
Carol:	Well – it fails in two important areas. I think I do want to move back to the real world outside university. I know academics are doing something worthwhile, but for a very narrow group of people. And I have to be realistic – even with a very good degree, my job prospects would be limited. But I still don't know what else I should do. What do *you* think I am suited for?
Adviser:	*(She is relying on me to come up with the answers again. I must be careful not to fall into the expert role and undermine her initial steps towards self-analysis and greater self-awareness.)*
	I did emphasise at the beginning that my role is to help you through the process of decision making and also that there are probably quite a number of jobs which you can do. The next step is to identify some of these so that you can begin to explore them in more detail. I can make some suggestions based on what we have discussed already and also show you how to find out more, but you will make good decisions for yourself at the end of the process of finding out about yourself and about jobs.

Carol: Yes. I know I have to do it for myself. It would be good if someone would just wave a magic wand ...

Adviser: I know. But we have to work in the real world. And you're much better equipped to do that now you've identified some important factors about what is important to you in a job. *Some* areas you could consider are in the fields of education – e.g. teaching, community education and careers work in schools; in local government – e.g. housing management, consumer adviser; with charitable bodies – e.g. as a fund raiser for a volunteer organisation; in the Health Service – on an administrative basis or in one of the medical therapies, such as speech therapy.

Carol: That's quite a list. And they would all satisfy those factors we identified?

THE ACTION-PLANNING PHASE

Adviser: To a greater or lesser extent. You will have to explore them in more detail and compare what they offer with the factors which are important to you. You should be aware that this is not a comprehensive list. I'm just giving you some examples of areas you could consider. We have a computer-aided guidance system which could help you to explore these areas and perhaps identify others. You might even want to change or add to the list of key factors you are looking for. What they all have in common is the need for further training of a vocational nature. Some of this can be on the job – for others you will need a postgraduate course – how do you feel about that?

Carol: Mixed, really, it all comes back to the funding, I suppose – if I didn't get it from the state, I think I would be prepared to borrow from Dad if I was convinced I could use the course to find a job.

Adviser: The other factor you should be aware of is the need to get some relevant practical experience before applying for a course.

Carol: Mmm. That sounds a good idea. What's the next step?

Adviser: Well, let's just review where we've got to. Could you just summarise how far you think we have reached?

Carol: Well, I think I'm clearer about the way I've been thinking about some of the factors which are important to me and I can see some areas of work that seem to fit along these lines. I think I've realised that I don't really want to do this particular postgraduate course after all. My reasons for applying were a bit confused.

Adviser: Yes, you seem to have done a lot of thinking and challenging of yourself today. I think the next step is to begin to firm up the key important factors for you and to explore some jobs in relation to these. You can do this by using the computer system I mentioned and following this up with further reading. Once you are clearer about the broad areas which interest you, it would be possible to visit a local contact in these areas or even consider gaining some voluntary experience. I'll show you details in the careers library.

The principal achievement of this careers interview has been to enable Carol to move from her anxious passivity about the guidance process, through a recognition of the losses inherent in moving on, to a much more constructive view of self and the world of work.

Chapter 11

Training and development for guidance practitioners

Training for guidance practitioners has undergone radical change in the 1990s. This chapter describes very briefly the nature of some of these changes and looks at the availability of training in the counselling approach to careers guidance. It also examines arrangements for the continuous professional development of careers advisers, especially in relation to the development of counselling skills.

FORMAL TRAINING

For careers officers

Training for careers officers is in an evolutionary state at the time of writing this book.[1] The long-term intention is to replace the Diploma in Careers Guidance with a National Vocational Qualification (NVQ). The original intention of the Advice, Guidance, Counselling & Psychotherapy Lead Body was to develop standards for core skills and evidence of competence across the whole range of occupations covered by the Lead Body. Its final conclusion, however, was that there would have to be separate 'evidence routes' to demonstrate how these core skills should be exhibited in individual occupations. The Lead Body is working closely with representatives of careers guidance practitioners to discover what evidence of competence should be accepted for careers officers. The fact that these standards have been drawn up by a Lead Body whose remit covers counselling as well as guidance should ensure that there is a heightened awareness of the links between counselling and guidance skills.

For careers advisers in higher education

It is not a prerequisite for careers advisers in higher education to have a specific qualification. A survey in the early 1990s showed that approximately half entered via the local authority Careers Service route and had a Diploma in Careers Guidance, while the remainder had come from a wide variety of backgrounds without formal guidance training, including personnel management, university administration, lecturing, being in the armed forces and information work.

For many years a training programme of short courses has been offered by the Association of Graduate Careers Advisory Services (AGCAS) at national and regional levels. Some of these focus on the skills and process of the guidance interview, while others offer more information-based training. Attendance at courses is optional and places on training courses are usually limited. The programme is not sequential and some courses happen on a 'one-off basis'. There are also variations around the country as to the level of activity in regional training groups.

In order to meet a growing demand for an appropriate qualification to meet the specific needs of careers staff in higher education, AGCAS in partnership with the University of Reading has introduced a Certificate and a Diploma in Careers Guidance in Higher Education. These qualifications are attained through a programme of core and optional modules, which include Foundation Guidance Skills and Guidance Skills. The modules are delivered via open learning methods which include workbooks, work-based assignments and short residential courses. Experienced practitioners can qualify for Accreditation of Prior Learning (APL) for up to 50 per cent of the course by submitting a portfolio of evidence of the competencies specified in the learning outcomes of the modules.

Because these qualifications have been designed to meet the broad criteria recommended by the Advice, Guidance, Counselling & Psychotherapy Lead Body, the Lead Body has recommended that there is not a pressing need for them to be replaced by NVQs in the first phase of the revision of the qualifications for guidance practitioners. AGCAS and Reading University are aware, however, of the need for the qualifications to address current issues and practice in higher education Careers Services, and the content of the modules is regularly revised to ensure its relevance to practitioners.

Counselling skills in careers guidance training

Some initial training provision for guidance practitioners incorporates both a counselling approach to guidance and training in counselling skills. Where training for the Diploma in Careers Guidance has been offered in the past, the emphasis on counselling skills within guidance has varied from one course to another, although the syllabus of every course had to satisfy the 'assessable core objectives' laid down in the guidelines for the training of careers officers. These included understanding theories of both guidance and counselling and 'the principles underlying effective interpersonal communication and their application to professional practice'.

Although the AGCAS/Reading qualifications do not include counselling as a specific element in the syllabus, there is an introduction to the use of counselling skills in the Guidance Skills and Foundation Guidance Skills modules, which are a compulsory element for careers advisers taking these courses.

Following such initial training, however, practice of the counselling approach to careers guidance needs to be maintained and developed through a lifelong process. Currently, in-service provision for this aspect of guidance work is limited in both the Careers Service and higher education Careers Services. Many motivated guidance practitioners, therefore, seek supplementary ways of developing their skills. Courses in counselling are now widely available at all levels, from a basic introduction to counselling skills to courses extending over a couple of years part-time. It is not possible to list courses in all forms of counselling throughout the UK, but the British Association for Counselling (see Useful addresses, p. 189) publishes a list of counselling courses in the various UK regions, together with a booklet on longer courses.

Counselling Skills and Advanced Counselling Skills have been included in recent programmes offered by the Institute of Careers Guidance to experienced careers officers throughout the UK. Attendance at such courses is optional and may depend on the extent of the training budget of individual Careers Services and other demands upon it.

Some of the counselling training provision which guidance practitioners use to develop their counselling skills relate to settings other than careers guidance, with emphasis on clients who are in some way disturbed. There are some instances of training in counselling skills being offered in short (one or half-day) courses, but there is a recognised need for further appropriate training in counselling skills over the whole guidance context. The National Institute for Careers Education & Counselling (NICEC) publishes annually a list of courses currently available for staff working in careers and educational guidance. This includes courses in counselling skills intended for guidance workers.[2]

The challenge for the trainers of careers advisers in both of these sectors is to ensure that the input on the counselling approach to guidance in initial training courses is of a sufficient depth and quality to enable careers advisers to recognise the distinct features of counselling in the context of their profession. This will encourage them to share their experience and continue to learn about good practice from one another through regular peer development, as described below. They will also be able to import concepts and practices from other counsellors and adapt these as required to fit the circumstances of counselling within a careers guidance context. Help from trainers in the structuring of such opportunities for 'cross-fertilisation' of ideas and the clarification of the desired learning outcomes from such exchanges will greatly aid the process of embedding counselling training within the careers guidance profession.

PEER GROUP SUPPORT

Although there are fewer formal arrangements for peer group support in Careers Services than in counselling generally, this can be set up informally either on an on-going basis or as the need arises. Support and, when the adviser feels safe enough, challenge from colleagues can greatly aid the learning process of using counselling in careers work using the following methods:

1 *Case study discussions* on a regular basis can help guidance practitioners to share good practice and to seek help in relationships with clients who are encountering problems. This can be done without breaching confidentiality by not disclosing the client's identity. This kind of discussion can take place on a one-to-one basis with a trusted colleague as an alternative to a group setting, although there may be less learning than in a group.

2 A further development from case studies is a *role play exercise* in which one can re-enact an interview which went badly, using

different words and strategies in order to effect an improvement, or can practise in anticipation of a forthcoming interview which is likely to be difficult. This exercise gives the adviser freedom to act the role of self or client – or both by turns – depending on the kind of insight which is required. This is a very flexible exercise, which can be used either with one other person or in a group.

3 *Observer learning* is a variant on role play, but in this instance the careers adviser seeking help simply explains the scenario and the nature of the problem and then remains on the sidelines as a silent observer while other members of the group either discuss or role play various options which could be explored to make progress in this situation. It can be extremely beneficial for an adviser who has reached stalemate with a client's problems to hear how other people would tackle them. Even confirmation that they too would find the problem difficult can be reassuring to an adviser who has experienced anxiety about the failure to produce a solution.

MENTORING

Another form of support and development for guidance practitioners is mentoring. This is a partnership in which a more experienced adviser acts as a sounding board and a facilitator in order to aid the professional development of a colleague. This support and encouragement enables the less experienced partner to work through any areas of difficulty in professional work and to receive feedback on proposals and performance. Although primarily intended as an aid to relatively new entrants to the profession, mentoring can also be adapted for use with peers on an equal footing.

Mentoring in the Careers Service

It is normal practice in Careers Services for a senior member of staff (e.g. assistant principal careers officer) to have responsibility for the training of probationer careers officers during the work-based year in which they complete Part II of the Local Government Management Board's two-year training programme. This may change if there are alterations in future training provision for careers officers, and in a few services a basic grade careers officer is appointed as a mentor for each probationer.

A recent pilot study[3] by the Department of Applied Social Studies at Paisley University examined the feasibility of more intensive supervision and mentoring of trainees by setting up an experimental mentoring scheme for Diploma in Careers Guidance students doing a work placement in area careers offices. It is debatable whether this is a true mentoring scheme, as the 'mentors' were also charged with assessing students' work and therefore could not be seen by the trainees as independent facilitators with no mixed motives. This experiment showed that a large majority of careers staff felt a more developed form of work-based mentoring was not feasible, given staffing constraints, pressure of work in the time available and their own lack of training in managing such a relationship. The conclusion was that a mentoring scheme for probationer careers officers was unlikely to be introduced in that region.

AGCAS mentoring scheme in higher education

When the Certificate and Diploma in Careers Guidance in Higher Education were introduced, AGCAS established a mentoring scheme to assist trainees. The intention of the mentoring scheme is to prevent isolation during the period of independent study.[4]

The scheme is voluntary in that trainees need not have mentors, while mentors are also volunteers and may be in the trainee's own Careers Service or an adjacent service. Feedback indicates that mentoring partnerships can work well in both settings if both partners have taken advantage of initial training, which is offered on a regional basis.

An additional advantage of mentoring is that the type of relationship built up between mentors and trainees is a good model for counselling, as it shares the following similarities:

1 Good mentoring should be led by the trainee rather than the mentor as the purpose is to encourage the trainee to realise his or her own potential within a supportive framework, so that the trainee will become more confident about using professional skills independently.
2 The mentor uses listening, empathy, summarising, reflecting back and other skills used by counsellors in order to facilitate a trainee's tentative exploration of difficult areas of practice.
3 The mentor in the scheme described here is not simultaneously an assessor for the qualification courses and so can be seen as

non-judgemental, while nevertheless offering constructive challenge as a positive contribution within the partnership. Some mentors, however, may be the line managers of their trainees and so be responsible for appraising their overall performance in a wider context. This issue is discussed in training and it is generally recommended that someone other than the trainee's head of service should be a mentor.

The scheme described in this section has potential for further development. As people who have benefited from good mentoring in the early years of their profession move into mainstream and senior posts, there may be more pressure for at least certain aspects of mentoring to be extended to all grades throughout the profession.

SUPERVISION AND CONTINUOUS PROFESSIONAL DEVELOPMENT

The use of the word 'supervision' in this context has a very specific meaning, referring not to the checking of work for accuracy, but to the offering of support with professional practice and a safety valve for the stress that can build up in any job calling for intensive interaction with people.

While this aspect of supervision is the primary area of need, the achievement of more extensive involvement of senior staff in the professional development of colleagues may be driven by a different stimulus. Many professions, including the closely allied field of personnel management, are moving towards a requirement for members to prove that they are keeping their skills and knowledge up to date by participating in a certain number of days of training or continuous professional development activities each year. The intention is that ultimately continuing membership of the professional body will depend upon practitioners' ability to prove their participation in such activities. When the value of such supervisory activity becomes more widely recognised, so also will the need for resources in this area.

At the moment neither the Institute of Careers Guidance nor the Association of Graduate Careers Advisory Services makes such a stipulation about membership, but the portfolio of accumulated evidence for accreditation of prior experience and learning for the Certificate and Diploma in Careers Guidance in

Higher Education and current developments towards Master's degrees in the management of guidance, which could operate partially on the same principle, suggest the beginnings of a move in this direction over the long term.

Provision of such evidence requires practitioners to be open to peers and senior colleagues observing their work and giving constructive feedback. This practice is currently not widespread in careers services, but if practitioners can be convinced of its beneficial aspects, then this could be adapted to provide the kind of supervisory support which is already mandatory for counsellors. Since few guidance practitioners have had extensive counselling training, there could be difficulty in arranging supervision for counselling skills in careers work by colleagues in their own careers service if this practice were to be adopted. Short-term measures to deal with this problem could include supervision by a counsellor external to the Careers Service or working with a self-help group of careers advisers currently engaged in counselling training, with some knowledge of supervision.

ADVICE, GUIDANCE, COUNSELLING & PSYCHOTHERAPY LEAD BODY

The establishment of a lead body of professional organisations in these allied fields to identify essential competencies for practitioners within its remit has created a forum for discussion and an opportunity for professionals in one area to find out about the work of people in other professions. The Lead Body's identification of a substantial number of core competencies shared by all of these professions has demonstrated how much these occupations have in common.

Although the Lead Body is charged exclusively with the identification and maintenance of standards of competence in these professions, the contacts which have been made during the Lead Body's negotiations have strengthened links among the various professional bodies. It is hoped that this cross-fertilisation will benefit professional practice through exchange of news on current developments and joint conferences on topics of mutual interest within the human relations field.

SUMMARY

Interest in training and continuous professional development in careers guidance has never been stronger, especially in the higher education sector. A poll conducted among AGCAS members in 1995 rated professional development as the issue of most concern to staff in higher education careers services. This stems from a recognition of the need for highly developed skills in order to deal effectively with the diverse range of needs of a wider group of clients and to meet the standards required by the 'quality culture' now developing in universities. This need is shared by other guidance practitioners in former local education authority careers services and the growing number of independent Careers Services.

Within this generally higher profile for training and development, many individual practitioners are seeking training in the use of counselling skills in a guidance context. As more advisers become trained in these skills, so the possibilities for regional training, peer group support and mentoring in this area will grow. The prognosis for the future development of the counselling approach within careers guidance is therefore promising.

Notes

1 INTRODUCTION TO COUNSELLING IN CAREERS GUIDANCE

1 McCormack, A., and Watson, A., unpublished occasional paper, Department of Human Resource Management, University of Strathclyde, Glasgow.

3 THEORETICAL BACKGROUND TO COUNSELLING

1 Rogers, C., 'The necessary and sufficient conditions of therapeutic personality change', *Journal of Counselling Psychology*, vol. 21, pp. 95–104.
2 Rogers, C., *Client-centred Therapy*, Boston, MA, Houghton Mifflin, 1957, pp. 498–503.
3 Carkhuff, R.R., *Helping and Human Relations*, vol. 2: *Practice and Research*, New York, Holt Rinehart and Winston, 1969, p. 47.
4 Egan, G., *The Skilled Helper: A Model for Systematic Helping and Inter-personal* Relating, Monterey, CA, Brooks Cole, 1975, pp. 28–54.
5 Super, D.E., The *Psychology of Careers*, New York, Harper and Row, 1957.
6 Adams, J., Hayes, J. and Hopson, B., *Transition*, London, Martin Robertson, 1976.
7 Berne, E., *Transactional Analysis* in Psychology, New York, Grove Press, 1961; *Games People Play*, New York, Grove Press, 1964; *What Do You Say after You Say Hello?*, London, Corgi Books, 1972.
8 Erikson, E., *Childhood and Society*, rev. edn., New York, W.W. Norton, 1963.
9 Levinson, D.J. *et al.*, The *Seasons of a Man's Life*, New York, A.A. Knopf, 1978.
10 Bandura, A., and Walters, R., *Social Learning and Personality Development*, New York, Holt, Rinehart and Wilson, 1963.
11 Mitchell, A.M., Jones, B. and Krumboltz, J., *Social Learning and Career Decision Making*, Carole Press, 1979.

12 Super, D. *et al.*, *Career Development Inventory*, Palo Alto, CA, Consulting Psychologists' Press, 1981.
13 Roberts, K., 'The social conditions, consequences and limitations of careers guidance', in *British Journal of Guidance and Counselling*, vol. 5, 1977.
14 Blau, P.M. *et al.*, 'Occupational choice: a conceptual framework', in *Industrial and Labour Relations Review*, vol. 9, pp. 531–43.
15 Law, W., 'Community interaction: a mid-range focus for theories of career development in young adults', in *British Journal of Guidance and Counselling*, vol. 9, no. 2, 1981, pp. 143–57.
16 Roger, A., *The Seven Point Plan*, London, National Institute of Industrial Psychology, 1952.

4 THE MODEL FOR A COUNSELLING APPROACH

1 Egan, G., *The Skilled Helper: A Systematic Approach to Effective Helping*, Monterey, CA, Brookes/Cole, 1990; Culley, S., *Integrative Counselling Skills in Action*, London, Sage, 1991.
2 Watts, A.G., 'Careers Education in Higher Education – Principles and Practice'. *British Journal of Guidance & Counselling*, vol. 5, no. 2, 1977.

5 COUNSELLING SKILLS

1 Culley, S., *Integrative Counselling Skills in Action*, London, Sage, 1991; Egan, G., *The Skilled Helper: A Systematic Approach to Effective Helping*, Monterey, CA, Brookes/Cole, 1990.

11 TRAINING AND DEVELOPMENT FOR GUIDANCE PRACTITIONERS

1 Staff development is the theme of the Spring 1995 edition of the *NICEC Careers Education & Guidance Bulletin*, National Institute for Careers Education & Counselling.
2 'Courses on careers education and guidance', in *NICEC Careers Education and Guidance Bulletin*, no. 44, Spring 1995.
3 McKay, L., 'Report on the Scottish Applications of Learning through Experience (SCALE) project for employment-based learning in careers guidance', University of Paisley, 1994.
4 Graham, B., *Mentoring and Professional Development*, Central Services Unit, Manchester, 1991; Graham, B., *Review of Mentoring in AGCAS*, Central Services Unit, 1994; Graham, B., 'Mentoring and Professional Development in Careers Services in higher education', in *British Journal of Guidance and Counselling*, vol. 22, no. 2, 1994.

Useful addresses

Advice, Guidance, Counselling & Psychotherapy Lead Body, Secretariat, 40a High Street, Welwyn, Herts AL6 9EQ.

Association of Graduate Careers Advisory Services (AGCAS), c/o Administration Manager, Careers Advisory Service, University of Sheffield, 8–10 Favell Road, Sheffield S10 2TN.

British Association for Counselling, 1 Regent Place, Rugby, Warwickshire CV21 2PJ.

British Psychological Society (Occupational Psychology Branch), St Andrew's House, 48 Princess Road East, Leicester LE1 4DR.

Institute of Careers Guidance, 27a Lower High Street, Stourbridge, West Midlands DY8 1TA.

Institute of Personnel & Development, IPD House, Camp Road, Wimbledon, London SW19 4UX.

National Association of Careers & Guidance Teachers, Portland House, 4 Bridge Street, Usk, Gwent NP5 1BG.

National Association for Educational Guidance for Adults, 1A Hilton Road, Milngavie, Glasgow G62 7DN.

National Institute for Careers Education & Counselling (NICEC), Sheraton House, Castle Park, Cambridge CB3 0AX.

Select bibliography

Ball, Ben, *Careers Counselling in Practice*, Brighton, Falmer Press, 1984.

Benjamin, Alfred, *The Helping Interview*, Burlington, MA, Houghton Mifflin, 1969.

British Journal of Guidance & Counselling, Cambridge, NICEC.

Careers Education & Guidance Bulletin, Cambridge, NICEC.

Culley, Sue, *Integrative Counselling Skills in Action*, London, Sage Publications, 1991.

Gothard, W.P., *Vocational Guidance: Theory and Practice*, London, Routledge & Kegan Paul, 1985.

Hawthorn, R., and Butcher, V., *Guidance Workers in the U.K.: Their Work and Training*, Cambridge, NICEC/CRAC, Hobsons Press, 1992.

Holdsworth, Ruth, *Psychology for Careers Counselling*, Basingstoke, Macmillan, 1982.

Hopson, Barrie, and Hayes, John, *The Theory and Practice of Vocational Guidance*, Oxford, Pergamon Press, 1968.

McLeod, J., *Introduction to Counselling*, Milton Keynes, Open University Press, 1993.

Nathan, Robert, and Hill, Linda, *Careers Counselling*, London, Sage Publications, 1992.

Nelson-Jones, Richard, *The Theory and Practice of Counselling Psychology*, London, Cassell, 1982.

Noonan, E., *Counselling Young People*, London, Methuen, 1990.

Weinrach, Stephen, *Career Counselling: Theoretical and Practical Perspectives*, Maidenhead, McGraw-Hill, 1979.

Index